MASTERING YOUR TIMEX SINCLAIR 1000™ PERSONAL COMPUTER

MASTERING YOUR TIMEX SINCLAIR 1000™ PERSONAL COMPUTER

Tim Hartnell
and
Dilwyn Jones

BANTAM BOOKS
TORONTO · NEW YORK · LONDON · SYDNEY

MASTERING YOUR TIMEX SINCLAIR 1000 ® PERSONAL COMPUTER

A Bantam Book / March 1983.

Timex Sinclair 1000 ® is a registered trademark
of the Timex Computer Corporation.

ISBN 0-553-23241-X

Published simultaneously in the United States and Canada

Bantam Books are published by Bantam Books, Inc. Its trademark, consisting of
the words ''Bantam Books'' and the portrayal of a rooster, is Registered in U.S.
Patent and Trademark Office and in other countries. Marca Registrada. Bantam
Books, Inc., 666 Fifth Avenue, New York, New York 10103.

PRINTED IN THE UNITED STATES OF AMERICA

O   0 9 8 7 6 5 4 3 2 1

CONTENTS

MASTERING YOUR TIMEX SINCLAIR 1000™ PERSONAL COMPUTER

FOREWORD

Your first hours with your new computer can be bewildering. Once you've run through the sample programs given in the manual, you're likely to think: "Yes, but now what?" This book is intended to answer that question. It will teach you everything you need to know about how to program your computer from first principles right up to quite sophisticated programming techniques. And while you're entering the programs, zapping aliens and asteroids all over the place, you'll discover that you're actually learning a lot about programming, and about computers in general—all without any effort at all.

This book is intended to be a tool, to be worked through with your computer turned on beside you. Its value will be greatly diminished if you simply try to read through the programs. It would be better to enter each program as you come to it, leaving no alien unzapped. That way, you'll gain the maximum benefit from the book, and you'll be a programming whiz before you know it.

It's time to get underway. Plug in your computer, turn on your TV, and let's get going.

INTRODUCTION
Finding your way around the keyboard

The first time you look at the T/S 1000 keyboard it is likely to cause some surprise. In addition to numbers and letters more or less where you would expect them to be on a typewriter keyboard, there seems to be a bewildering collection of odd symbols and words on the keys, with other words above and below the keys. Trying to figure out how to get what you want from a key—and some keys can produce as many as five different results—can seem very difficult. But it is not.

The computer is designed so that it knows, more often than not, which of the five possibilities you will need. And when the computer cannot tell from the context of what you're typing which part of the key's possibilities you want, it is very easy to instruct it. Plug in your T/S 1000 as shown in the manual which came with your computer. An inverse K (a white K on a little black square) will appear in the bottom left-hand corner. This is called the cursor, and it is the key to working out which possibility you'll get when you press a key. If the cursor is a K, you'll get numbers or *keywords* (the words in white above the keys). We'll look at keywords, and the other possibilities, in more detail shortly. If the cursor is an inverse L, the keyboard works more or less like a typewriter. That is, you press the S key, and the letter S appears on the screen. The other two possibilities for the cursor are an F (function mode) or a G (graphics mode).

The SHIFT key (the one with the word SHIFT in red, in the bottom left-hand corner of the keyboard) allows you to get the words and symbols written in red on the keys, as you'll see in a moment.

SLOW/FAST

When you first turn on the computer, it is in SLOW mode. In SLOW mode, looking after the smoothness of the television picture is considered more important than "thinking," so the computer does its thinking between sending picture information to the television. The programs in this book are designed to be run in SLOW mode, so the computer is in the correct mode for running them automatically. In FAST mode, the computer's thinking is considered more important than looking after the picture, which can become very jerky.

However, it is much easier to enter a program into the computer when it is in FAST mode, so we need to be able to switch between the modes at will—FAST to get a program into the computer, SLOW for running it.

As I said, the computer is in SLOW mode automatically when you turn it on. To get into FAST mode, press on the SHIFT key (remember, it's in the bottom left-hand corner of the keyboard), then press the F key (which, as you'll see, has the word FAST written on it in red). The word FAST should appear on the screen. Now press the ENTER key (second from the bottom, on the right-hand side), and you'll see the screen jump, and the *message* Ø/Ø appear in the bottom left-hand corner of the screen. This message—Ø/Ø—means "all OK."

Now press any key, and you'll see the display jumping about. This is what FAST mode looks like—far less attractive to watch, but easier to use for program entry.

You may find, when you write your own programs, that the speed of SLOW is, in fact, too slow for your liking. This can happen when the computer must do a great deal of work to determine an answer, and in this sort of program—when the display is less important than getting a quick answer—you should run your programs in FAST. However, for many programs (such as the ones in this book) the T/S 1000 is still fast enough in SLOW for our needs.

To get back into SLOW mode from FAST, hold down the

SHIFT key again, then press the D key (where the word SLOW is written in red). The display will *lock on*, and the "all OK" message will appear on the screen. From now on, we'll assume that you have your computer in FAST mode when you enter programs, and in SLOW mode when you run them.

Keywords

The words written in white *above* many of the keys are keywords. These are the fundamental words from which programs are built. When you write a program, as we'll discuss in more detail shortly, you start with a number (the line number), then follow this with a keyword, and then, generally, some additional material.

Here's an example to make it clear. Make sure your computer is *empty*. You can do this by turning off the power, waiting a few seconds, then turning it on again. This is not the best way to clear the contents of the computer's memory (the word NEW above the A key is designed to do it), but this method is the simplest at this stage.

Once the computer is empty, type in the number 10. It will sit down at the bottom of the screen. The 10 is a line number, an idea which will be discussed in a little more detail shortly. Now press the P key, and you'll see the word PRINT appear on the screen, just after the 10. The keywords appear automatically after a line number. Now press ENTER and you'll see the program line move up to the top of the screen, which means it has been accepted by the computer.

Functions

Functions are the words in white *under* many of the keys. You'll meet functions (such as LEN, INKEY$, and AT) many times in this book. You get into the *function mode* (when the inverse K cursor turns into an inverse F) by holding down the SHIFT key, and then pressing the ENTER key, which you can see has the word FUNCTION on it in red, above the word ENTER. When you do this, you'll see the cursor has turned into an inverse F. Now press the C key, and the word AT should appear on the screen. Try the B key (to get the word INKEY$) and the P key (to get TAB).

Operators

The operators are link and comparison words and symbols like THEN, AND, TO, and <>. You get these by holding down the SHIFT key, then pressing the key for the operator you want. Clear the computer as before, then hold down the SHIFT key and press U. The dollar sign should appear. Press 2 and you'll get the word AND, 3 for THEN, and 4 for TO.

The word in red on the 1 key—EDIT—has a special function. It is used to bring a line down from the top of the screen (where it has been accepted into the computer's memory as part of a program) to the bottom of the screen so you can change or edit it in some way.

To show this in action, clear the computer, then type in the following:

```
10 PRINT 6
```

Press ENTER and this line will move to the top of the screen. Now hold down the SHIFT key, and press the 1 key, and the line will reappear at the bottom of the screen. Still holding down the SHIFT, press the 8 key (where you'll see a little arrow pointing to the right), and you'll see the cursor move across the word PRINT to rest between it and the 6. Press the 8 key again (still holding down SHIFT), and the cursor will jump over the 6. The word DELETE is on the Ø key (note that the zero has a line through it to distinguish it from the letter O). Still holding down SHIFT, press the Ø key once, and the number 6 will be erased. Take your finger off the SHIFT, and press the 5 key, to see the number 5 appear at the end of the line. What you have at the bottom of the screen should look like this:

```
10 PRINT 5
```

Now press ENTER, and the line will appear at the top of the screen, taking the place of the previous one.

Graphics

The final mode we'll discuss is the graphics mode.

Clear the computer's memory with NEW (SHIFT, then press the A key so the word NEW appears, then press ENTER). Now type in the number 10, then press the P key, so the keyword PRINT appears. You should have this at the bottom of the screen:

```
10 PRINT
```

Now hold down the SHIFT key, and press the P again, and a pair of quote marks will appear. Still holding down SHIFT, press the 9 key, and the cursor will turn into a G, meaning the computer is in the graphics mode. Now type in the word TEST, and you'll see it appears in white letters on little black squares, rather than in black letters on the ordinary white background. Holding down the SHIFT again, press the 9 key again, and the inverse G will turn back into an L. Still holding down SHIFT, press the P key for the closing quote marks. Now press ENTER and the following line should appear at the top of the screen:

```
10 PRINT "▚▚▚▚"
```

Run this program (by pressing the R key to get the word RUN at the bottom of the screen, then pressing the ENTER key), and the word TEST, in white letters on a little black background strip, will appear at the top of the screen. If you are in the graphics mode, and you hold down the SHIFT key while pressing many of the keys, instead of an inverse letter, you'll get the little patterns and designs on the keys. These can be used to build up pictures.

We've now covered the basic handling of the keyboard. We do not expect that you'll understand all of this instantly. You will, from time to time, have to refer back to this section. You should, however, quickly master the fundamentals of the keyboard, and the need to refer to this introductory section will diminish as time goes on. We suggest you read through this section again before continuing.

CHAPTER 1
The PRINT statement

PRINT is probably the most-used command in BASIC. It is the command which allows the computer to communicate with you. Type the following line into your computer, and then press ENTER:

```
PRINT 5
```

You'll see that the computer obediently prints the number 5. You can use the PRINT command to make your computer act as a calculator. Enter the following, and then press ENTER:

```
PRINT 5-3
```

When you press ENTER, you'll see it prints up the correct result. This *direct calculation mode* can work out problems as complex as you wish. Try the following, remembering to press ENTER after you've done so to make the computer act on what you've typed in:

```
PRINT SQR (8+1)
```

This asks the computer to PRINT the square root (that's what SQR means) of the sum of the numbers in parentheses, that is, the square root of 9. If your computer is functioning correctly, you should—of course—get an answer of 3.

So you can see that PRINT can be used in the direct mode to print out numbers and the results of calculations. It can also print out words. Type the following, then press ENTER:

```
PRINT HI THERE
```

Instead of happily printing HI THERE, the computer comes up with what is called an error message. In this case, the

7

error message reads 2/Ø, meaning that a variable has not been found. If you want the computer to print out words, the words must be enclosed within quotation marks. Enter and run (that is, press ENTER after typing in) the following:

```
PRINT "HI THERE"
```

You'll see the words HI THERE appear at the top of the screen.

To recap quickly, simply used as a command, PRINT 2 + 3 will tell the computer to print out the result of that addition. Entering PRINT "WORDS" will get the computer to print out everything which is within the quote marks.

Computers use programs, and it is now time to write our first, simple program. Enter and run this program. When you run this, which you do by pressing the R key, and then pressing ENTER, you should see a printout similar to that which is below the program listing.

```
10 REM PROGRAM ONE
20 PRINT "THIS IS A DEMONSTRAT
ION"
30 PRINT 1
40 PRINT 2
50 PRINT "THIS IS THE END"

THIS IS A DEMONSTRATION
1
2
THIS IS THE END
```

While we have this program in the computer, let's learn a little more about programs. Enter the word LIST (which you do by pressing the K key), and then press ENTER. You'll see that the program listing comes back. Notice that every line starts with a line number. The first line, in this case numbered 1Ø, starts with the word REM. REM is computer talk for *remark*. It is used in a program when you want to explain what is going on within that program, or what program it is (as in this case), so that when you return to it later, you'll know what is going on. The computer ignores REM statements when it comes to them.

A REM statement is made up of a line number, then the word REM, and some text. The message which follows the word REM can be made up from anything you like—letters, numbers, punctuation marks, graphics, or spaces—although it is best to keep the messages as brief and clear as you can. Although anything typed after the word REM is ignored by the computer when it is running a program, a REM line still uses up memory.

REM statements are often like the following:

```
10 REM THIS WORKS OUT THE SCORE
10 REM FIND THE ANGLE
```

There is no reason why there should be just one REM statement, but if the commentary you wish to add to a particular line of a program is one which may take up more than one line of text, it is important to place the word REM at the beginning of each new line. For example:

```
60 REM THE MULTIPLICATION
      ROUTINE IN WHICH
70 REM THE TWO VARIABLES
      A AND B
80 REM ARE MULTIPLIED TOGETHER
```

So long as each REMark line starts with the word REM, the computer will ignore the text that follows on that line (although the complete program listing, REMs and all, will be printed on the screen if a LIST is requested).

Now, let's have a look at editing. Type in the number 10, then press ENTER, press LIST, and press ENTER again. You'll see your program reappear as follows. Line 10 has disappeared. It is very easy to get rid of lines you don't want in a computer just by typing in the relevant line number and then pressing ENTER.

```
10 REM
20 PRINT "THIS IS A DEMONSTRAT
ION"
30 PRINT 1
40 PRINT 2
50 PRINT "THIS IS THE END"
```

You'll recall, from the times you've pressed LIST while working through this section, that LIST is the BASIC command which we use to get the computer to print out the entire program it is currently holding. All the lines in the program are LISTed in numerical order, rather than in the order in which they were entered into the computer. That is, the computer automatically sorts its lines into order. Type in the following, and then press ENTER.

```
15 PRINT "THIS IS A NEWLINE"
```

You'll see, in the next program, that the new line (15) automatically moves to its correct position within the listing.

```
10 REM
15 PRINT "THIS IS A NEWLINE"
20 PRINT "THIS IS A DEMONSTRAT
ION"
30 PRINT 1
40 PRINT 2
50 PRINT "THIS IS THE END"
```

As you've no doubt realized, the RUN command is used to start the computer operating on a program which you have entered into the computer, either by typing it in, or by loading a program in from a cassette. The computer executes all the lines stored in its memory, starting from the lowest number, and working through in order. Various commands can make the computer loop back on itself, but in essence the computer works through a program in line number order, unless told to do otherwise.

If you want the program to stop at a particular point, you can use—naturally enough—a command called STOP. Type in 25 STOP (from the A key, while holding down SHIFT), then press ENTER, then run the program. It will print out:

```
THIS IS A NEWLINE

THIS IS A DEMONSTRATION
```

Then, at the bottom of the screen, will be the message 9/25, which means a STOP was executed at line 25.

We'll return to look at PRINT in a little more detail later on, but there is one more command I'd like to introduce now. The command NEW will erase any program from the computer's memory, and should always be used to remove anything from the memory before you start writing a new program. If you don't do this, and you use different line numbers for the second program, you'll find the new lines may well be interwoven with the lines from the old program. The NEW command is brutal, and final, causing the computer to dramatically forget everything you had typed in, or loaded in from tape.

Try it now on your computer. Type in NEW (from the A key), press ENTER, then press LIST and press ENTER again. You'll find, not unexpectedly, that no listing appears. Try LIST 10, and you'll get the same result.

PRINT formatting and TAB

To continue our exploration of the PRINT command, enter and run the next program.

```
10  REM PRINT FORMATS
20  PRINT
30  PRINT
40  PRINT
50  PRINT
55  PRINT "HI ";55
70  PRINT ,"HI ";70
80  PRINT 12
90  PRINT 1,2
100 PRINT ,1
110 PRINT ,1;2
```

Follow this explanation carefully, and you should learn a lot about the way the computer formats its print output. You can then use what you've learned to arrange output of your own programs as you wish. I'll go through the program line by line:

10   Title of the program. This is shown as a REM statement.

20–50   Each of these PRINTs, with nothing following, prints a blank line, moving the next print position down a line. This explains the gap at the top of the screen when you run the program.

55   This prints the word HI and then, leaving a space, prints the number 55, so you know which line it comes from.

70   The comma (SHIFT the period, near the bottom right-hand corner of the keyboard), as you can see, moves the start of the line halfway across the screen.

80   This allows the numbers 1 and 2 to be printed close together. Note that even if there is a space between

the numbers in the program (as in PRINT 1   2), the computer will still print them as 12.

90   This line uses commas between the numbers to ensure that they will be printed in separate halves of the screen.

100   The comma at the beginning of the line moves the 1 halfway across the screen, just as the word HI was moved in line 70.

110   The semicolon between the numbers ensures that they are printed hard up against each other, just as they were in line 80.

You can use the comma and semicolon within PRINT statements to produce the screen display you need. Clear the program with NEW, then enter and run the next series of programs, to produce a number of effects.

The first program, called PRINT TWO, simply prints the numbers 1 to 10 down the side of the screen. The next one (PRINT TWO - B) prints them hard up against each other. PRINT TWO - C prints them in neat little columns, and PRINT TWO - D prints out the numbers, again from 1 to 10, with a single space between them.

As we mentioned at the beginning of the book, there are a number of operator and link words which are printed in red on the keyboard. You get these by holding down the SHIFT key, then pressing the corresponding key. In line 20 of the next four programs you will see the word TO. You get this by holding down SHIFT, and pressing the 4 key.

```
10 REM PRINT TWO
20 FOR J=1 TO 10
30 PRINT J
40 NEXT J

10 REM PRINT TWO - B
20 FOR J=1 TO 10
30 PRINT J;
40 NEXT J

10 REM PRINT TWO - C
20 FOR J=1 TO 10
30 PRINT J,
40 NEXT J

10 REM PRINT TWO - D
20 FOR J=1 TO 10
30 PRINT J;" ";
40 NEXT J
```

CHAPTER 2
The use of TAB

TAB (for tabulate) is a command which can usefully be combined with PRINT. It moves the PRINT position across the number of spaces specified following the number. Enter programs PRINT TWO - E and PRINT TWO - F and see the effect of the TAB command in these.

```
10 REM PRINT TWO - E
20 FOR J=1 TO 10
30 PRINT TAB J;J
40 NEXT J
```

```
10 REM PRINT TWO - F
20 FOR J=1 TO 10
30 PRINT TAB 3*J;J
40 NEXT J
```

Our next program shows TAB in use. When you run the program, you'll be asked to enter a number under 30. Enter a positive integer (that is, do not enter 3.4 or 7.65) and you'll see the "X" printed with your number of spaces in front of it. Run this for a while, then stop it by entering any *letter* except A. (Note, by the way, that SCROLL is on the B key, and it has the effect of moving the PRINT position to the bottom of the screen, moving everything already on the screen up by one line.)

```
10 REM TAB DEMONSTRATION
20 SCROLL
30 PRINT "GIVE ME A NUMBER UND
ER 30"
40 INPUT A
50 SCROLL
60 PRINT TAB A;"X"
70 SCROLL
80 PRINT "THE X IS PRINTED WIT
H ";A
```

```
  90 SCROLL
 100 PRINT "SPACES IN FRONT OF I
T"
 110 SCROLL
 120 GOTO 20
```

CHAPTER 3
SAVEing programs

You may wish to keep a permanent copy of any of your programs. You can save programs by typing in the program, connecting up your cassette recorder as shown in the manual, then typing in SAVE followed by the name of the program within quote marks. Turn your cassette recorder on to "record," after connecting it up as shown in the manual, and then press the ENTER key.

We suggest you make a habit of saving each program three times in a row, on a C-12 or C-15 (i.e., computer) cassette, and that you only put one program on each side of a tape. Label the tape clearly with the load name. Although it may seem wasteful to use up a whole side of a cassette with just one program recorded three times, the frustration you will save yourself by not having to search through tape after tape for a program you want will more than compensate for using more cassettes than is strictly necessary. The program is recorded three times just in case the tape gets damaged at some point, or you accidentally erase part of the program, or—as sometimes happens—one recording of the program refuses to load properly.

You should clean the recorder's heads frequently, using liquid, not a tape cleaner ribbon in a cassette, to ensure that the clearest possible signal is put onto the tape.

Getting programs back into the computer can prove difficult at times. If you do have LOAD problems then try the following tips:

1. Disconnect the lead not in use from both the computer and the cassette recorder.
2. Try operating the cassette recorder from batteries.

3. Try moving the computer and the cassette recorder further apart, as well as the TV if you can.

4. Change the volume setting on the cassette recorder, since some cassettes may have a higher output than others. Try changing the tone control setting, in particular turn up the treble or turn down the bass.

5. Make sure your leads have not broken or cracked, or a solder joint has not come loose.

6. The memory of computers is measured in a unit called K (which stands for kilobyte, 1024 characters). Your T/S 1000 is supplied with 2K of memory when you buy it, and this is enough memory for many applications (and for all but a few of the programs in this book). However, you may find eventually that you want more memory, and you can then buy a 16K RAMPACK to plug into the back of the computer. Do not try loading a 2K program SAVEd using a RAMPACK because, although the program itself might easily fit into 2K, the display file will be at its full size so there will be no room for everything in the computer. If you've got a program saved using a RAMPACK and the program won't load, then beg, steal, borrow, or even buy a RAMPACK, and go through the motions described above and resave the program to make it suitable for loading into 2K in the future.

7. This sounds silly, but make sure your plugs are in the correct hole! You may find it useful to stick labels on top of the computer above the sockets to tell you which one is which so that you don't have to peer around the side to check this every time.

Now, let's return to TAB. We can only use TAB with a single number after the word. Remember, TAB A will move the start of the PRINT position A + 1 spaces across a line. You can have the word PRINT followed by AT, and two numbers, such as PRINT AT 10, 6; which will move the PRINT position 6 spaces across and 10 down. The top left-hand corner of the screen is 0, 0, so PRINT AT Ø, Ø; indicates that the printing will begin in the top left-hand corner of the screen. The left-hand side of the screen is numbered 0, while the right-hand side is 31. The screen is 32 characters wide, so the position furthest to the right is numbered 31.

PRINT AT

The following program shows PRINT AT in action, positioning an X at the position you choose. When you run the program, the computer will wait for you to enter a number. The first number you enter will be the first number after the word AT, and this number is the number of lines (plus one) at which you'll be printing. That is, if you entered 5, the computer would move to the sixth line down. The T/S 1000 will wait for another number, which is like the TAB number, that is, it is the number of spaces across the screen which will be in front of that which you are printing. If you entered 5 for this second number, you'd see an X appear on the screen six lines down, and in the sixth position across (that is, with five spaces in front of it). The program will print up at the top the location at which the X is printed.

Run this for a while, then terminate it by entering any letter except A or B.

```
10 REM PRINT AT DEMONSTRATION
20 INPUT A
25 CLS
30 INPUT B
40 PRINT AT 0,0;"THIS SHOWS PR
INT AT ";A;",";B
50 PRINT AT A,B;"X"
60 GOTO 20
```

```
THIS SHOWS PRINT AT 4,12



                    X
```

CHAPTER 4
GOTO

One important ability in programming is to be able to branch to different parts of the program during execution. Without this, the program would always run from the lowest line number to the highest, and then stop. One statement which allows you to move around the program at will is GOTO. The GOTO statement consists of a line number followed by the word GOTO and another line number, or followed by a calculation (such as GOTO 2*X, or GOTO 200+340).

If the computer came across 140 GOTO 190, it would jump immediately from line 140 to line 190. This is called an *unconditional branch*. That is, it is a jump that does not depend on the existence of any condition. Once at line 190, the program continues to execute in order, until it comes to the end, or comes to another line directing it somewhere else.

You can use GOTO to produce programs which run almost forever. These can be quite effective, especially at the end of a game. Run the following to see this in action:

```
10 PRINT "YOU HAVE WON ";
20 GOTO 10
```

CHAPTER 5
Random numbers

Random numbers are very useful for playing games. Let's examine the production of random numbers, and use them in a few simple programs.

The computer allows you to generate what are called *floating point numbers* between 0 and 1. A floating point number is one which contains a decimal point (such as 0.2341 or 43.65) rather than integers, or whole numbers (such as 12, 666 or 26753).

Enter and run the following to see a range of numbers (floating point numbers, as you'll see) between 0 and 1. You get RND from the T key, after going into the function mode.

```
10 PRINT RND
20 GOTO 10
```

You'll get a list of numbers something like this:

```
0.34892273
0.16993713
0.74623108
0.96762085
0.57159424
0.87005615
0.25434876
.07699585
0.77574158
0.18086243
0.56561279
0.42144775
0.60923767
0.89326782
```

You'll find that random integers are often of far more use than are the numbers between 0 and 1. To do this, enter a statement like INT (RND*30) + 1. Run this program.

You're likely to get a series of numbers such as those following
the program.

```
10 REM RANDOM INTEGERS
20 LET A=INT (RND*100)+1
30 SCROLL
40 PRINT TAB 8;A
50 GOTO 20
```

```
        88
        26
         8
        78
        19
        57
        43
        61
        70
       100
        66
        34
        28
        72
        52
        39
        64
        37
        40
```

The computer takes the number in brackets (known as the
argument of the function) and selects numbers at random
between 1 and that number. To get negative random numbers, just put a minus sign in front of the word INT. Try that,
and run it again, to get a result like this:

```
       -40
       -89
       -55
       -35
       -47
       -69
        -5
       -72
       -23
       -57
       -85
       -17
       -74
       -65
       -17
       -86
```

You can use the random numbers for any application where you need to emulate a random activity in the real world, like the distribution of weeds in a garden, the spread of clouds in the sky, or the result of rolling dice. The next program emulates the roll of a six-sided die. Enter and run it a few times.

```
10 REM * DICE ROLLER *
20 PRINT "HOW MANY TIMES WILL"
30 PRINT "I ROLL THE DIE?"
40 INPUT A
50 CLS
60 PRINT "RESULT OF ROLLING TH
E DIE",A;" TIMES:"
70 FOR B=1 TO A
80 LET C=INT (RND*6)+1
90 PRINT ,C
100 NEXT B
```

```
RESULT OF ROLLING THE DIE
7 TIMES:
                    1
                    5
                    1
                    3
                    2
                    5
                    6
```

While the theoretical distribution of numbers between 1 and 6 with a six-sided die suggests that each number has an equal chance of coming up in a long, long series of rolls, the totals produced when you use two dice approach the following distribution:

TOTAL SHOWING	NO. OF WAYS IT CAN BE THROWN	PROBABILITY	PERCENTAGE
2	1	1/36	2.77
3	2	2/36,1/18	5.55
4	3	3/36,1/12	8.33
5	4	4/36,1/9	11.11
6	5	5/36	13.88
7	6	6/36,1/6	16.66
8	5	5/36	13.88
9	4	4/36,1/9	11.11
10	3	3/36,1/12	8.33
11	2	2/36,1/18	5.55
12	1	1/36	2.77

To test just how random the random number generator is, enter and run the following program, which rolls two dice as many times as you request.

```
10 REM   * TWO DICE *
20 PRINT "HOW MANY TIMES WILL
I","ROLL THE DICE?"
30 INPUT D
40 CLS
50 DIM A(12)
60 FOR C=1 TO D
70 LET DIE1=INT (RND*6)+1
80 LET DIE2=INT (RND*6)+1
90 PRINT AT 3,2;"THE DICE FELL
";DIE1;" ";DIE2;" TOTAL ";DIE1+
DIE2;" "
100 LET SUM=DIE1+DIE2
110 LET A(SUM)=A(SUM)+1
120 FOR B=2 TO 12
130 PRINT AT B+3,5;B;" ",A(B);"
";INT (A(B)/C*100);" PER CENT "
140 NEXT B
150 NEXT C
```

Here's the result of one run when I got the computer to roll the two dice 60 or so times. The top two figures (5 and 6) are the result of the current roll. Next, from there down, the numbers 2 to 12 in the left-hand column are the totals we are looking for, followed by the number of times that total has been rolled in the current run. The final column shows the approximate percentage distribution of each of the totals.

```
THE DICE FELL 5 6 TOTAL 11

     2              3  4 PER CENT
     3              2  3 PER CENT
     4              5  7 PER CENT
     5              3  4 PER CENT
     6              7 11 PER CENT
     7             12 19 PER CENT
     8              7 11 PER CENT
     9              9 14 PER CENT
    10              5  8 PER CENT
    11              3  4 PER CENT
    12              6  9 PER CENT
```

You can see that this run is starting to approach the theoretical distribution, which suggests the random number generator is performing its task properly. The numbers produced are not totally random, but are from a very long list of numbers, which is so long that no pattern can be discerned.

Bull fight

Here's a very simple game which shows the random number generator in action. The game is not really much of a game, but entering and running it is well worthwhile. Once you've played a few rounds of the game, return to this book for a discussion of the program. You should be pleasantly surprised at how much you have already learned.

You are a matador. The bull will charge you 10 times. You select a number between 1 and 3, and the bull does the same. So long as the numbers are different, you survive that move. If the bull picks the same number, the game is over. You are given a score at the end.

```
    THE BULL IS CHARGING

WHICH MOVEMENT? (1 TO 3)

YOU ARE SAFE IN MOVE 1

THE BULL PICKED 2

YOU PICKED 1
```

```
   10 REM BULLFIGHT
   20 LET SCORE=0
   30 FOR G=1 TO 10
   40 PRINT AT 4,4;"THE BULL IS C
HARGING"
   50 PRINT
   60 PRINT "WHICH MOVEMENT? (1 T
O 3)"
   70 INPUT A
   80 IF A<1 OR A>3 THEN GOTO 70
   90 LET B=INT (RND*3)+1
  100 IF A=B THEN GOTO 220
  110 PRINT
  120 PRINT "YOU ARE SAFE IN MOVE
";G
  130 PRINT
  140 PRINT "THE BULL PICKED ";B
  150 PRINT
  160 PRINT "YOU PICKED ";A
  170 FOR H=1 TO 20
```

```
 180 NEXT H
 190 CLS
 200 NEXT G
 210 GOTO 230
 220 PRINT "YOU HAVE FAILED AS A
","MATADOR"
 230 PRINT
 240 PRINT "YOU SCORED ";100*(G-
1)
```

Let's go through the program line by line:

10	REM statement title.
20	Sets the variable SCORE to equal zero. We'll be discussing variables shortly.
30	Starts the FOR/NEXT loop to count the 10 goes. FOR/NEXT loops are discussed a little later in the book.
40	Prints out that the bull is charging.
50	Blank PRINT line.
60	Asks the player to enter a number between 1 and 3.
70	Accepts the number from the player.
80	Checks to see if the number lies between 1 and 3, and if it does not, goes back to line 70 to accept another input from the player.
90	Sets B equal to the bull's number, a number chosen at random between 1 and 3.
100	Compares the player's number (A) with the bull's number (B) and if they are the same, sends action to line 220 to tell you you have failed as a matador.
110	Blank PRINT line.
120	Tells the player he or she has survived that move.
130	Blank PRINT line.
140	Tells the player the bull's number.
150	Blank PRINT line.
160	Reminds player of his or her number.
170–180	Puts in a short delay before next round.
190	Clears the screen.
200	Goes back for the next round.
210	If the player has survived 10 rounds, goes to print out the score.
220	This failure message appears if A and B were found to be equal in line 100.
230	Blank PRINT line.
240	Prints out the score.

Reading through this explanation a couple of times, and looking carefully at the line or lines it refers to, should teach you quite a bit more about programming. There are a number of specific commands which we will look at in more detail, but you're probably starting to pick up quite a bit at this stage.

CHAPTER 6
Variables

You will have noticed in the previous program that letters were used to represent numbers. The letter A was assigned (in line 7Ø) to a number between 1 and 3 and B was assigned in the same way in line 9Ø. The letters A and B in this program are called variables.

There are two types of variables: numeric and string (alphanumeric). Almost any combination of letters and numbers can be used as a variable, so long as it begins with a letter and there are no punctuation marks or symbols within the name. So SMUDGEPOT and D17 are valid variable names, while 2SMUDGE and 1D7 are not. Numeric variables, letters or combinations of letters, and numbers beginning with a letter, are simple to use. You can assign a variable of this type to any number within the computer's numerical range.

By the way, as you probably know, the computer uses scientific notation to display large numbers, with the number as a single digit and up to eight decimal places, followed by the letter E (for exponentiation) and the power of 10 to which the number is to be multiplied. Enter and run the following demonstration which shows the variable A in use, being assigned to a number which is being multiplied repeatedly by 10, and then printed.

```
10 REM SCIENTIFIC NOTATION
20 LET A=1234
25 SCROLL
30 PRINT A
40 LET A=10*A
50 GOTO 25
```

```
1234
12340
123400
1234000
```

```
12340000
123400000
1234000000
12340000000
123400000000
1234000000000
1.234E+13
1.234E+14
1.234E+15
1.234E+16
1.234E+17
1.234E+18
1.234E+19
1.234E+20
1.234E+21
1.234E+22
1.234E+23
```

Note that after the number has 13 digits (1234000000000) it is printed as a number, a decimal point, more numbers after the decimal point, the letter E, and a power of 10. Try and predict how long this program will run until it exceeds the maximum number possible on the computer, then run it until it crashes to see if you were right.

Looking at the listing tells us more of things about variables. The variable is assigned by just entering the name of the variable (in this case, A), preceded by the word LET, and followed by an equals sign and the value which we want assigned to the variable. If we said LET A = 99, then following this with PRINT A would produce 99. Line 40 looks a little odd. The asterisk (*) stands for multiply in BASIC. Line 40 seems to be saying that A is equal to 10 times itself, which—in terms of standard arithmetic—is not true. This is, however, the way the assignment (LET) statement is used in BASIC.

String variables

String variables are represented by a letter followed by a dollar sign. Type LET A$ = "HELLO", press ENTER, then type PRINT A$, and press ENTER. This will give you HELLO. You can put anything, including numbers, symbols, punctuation marks, and letters within the quotation marks, to be assigned to a string variable. A series of letters and whatever, within quote marks in this way, is known as a string.

Crickets

There is, strange to say, a correlation between the temperature and the number of times a cricket chirps each minute. The following program converts the number of chirps per minute into temperature, in degrees Fahrenheit. Enter and run it a few times. Note that the variable chirp is set equal initially to 80 in line 20. This is converted into the variable temperature in line 30, and this latter variable is used in the PRINT statement in line 40. The variable chirp is incremented by a random number between 1 and 7 in line 60, there is a short delay (lines 70 and 80) and then the program returns to line 30 to go through the whole process again. It will run for a long, long time (until you exceed the highest possible number the computer can cope with) if you do not interrupt its running with the BREAK key.

```
THE TEMPERATURE IS 60
WHEN THERE ARE 80 CHIRPS

THE TEMPERATURE IS 61
WHEN THERE ARE 84 CHIRPS

THE TEMPERATURE IS 63
WHEN THERE ARE 90 CHIRPS

THE TEMPERATURE IS 63
WHEN THERE ARE 92 CHIRPS

THE TEMPERATURE IS 64
WHEN THERE ARE 94 CHIRPS
```

```
  10 REM CHIRP CONVERTER
  20 LET CHIRP=80
  30 LET TEMPERATURE=INT ((CHIRP
/4)+40.5)
  35 SCROLL
  40 PRINT "THE TEMPERATURE IS "
;TEMPERATURE
  45 SCROLL
  50 PRINT "WHEN THERE ARE ";CHI
RP;" CHIRPS"
  60 LET CHIRP=CHIRP+INT (RND*7)
+1
  70 FOR J=1 TO 10
  80 NEXT J
  90 SCROLL
 100 GOTO 30
```

Although it takes a little longer to type in long variable names, these have a clear advantage over use of names like A, B, and C2. It is easier to remember, without having to refer back, what each variable represents. Here is another program which uses two variable names to help make clear what is going on. Enter and run this.

```
10 REM ** VARIABLES **
20 LET W$="THE NUMBER IS "
30 LET NUMBER=3
40 PRINT
50 PRINT W$;NUMBER
55 PRINT
60 PRINT "THE SQUARE OF ";NUMB
ER
70 PRINT TAB 5;"IS ";NUMBER*NU
MBER
75 PRINT
80 PRINT "AND THE SQUARE ROOT"
90 PRINT "IS ";SQR (NUMBER)
```

To summarize:

•Numeric variable: This can have any name, so long as it starts with a letter and does not contain punctuation or symbols.

•String variable: This is a letter followed by a dollar sign, which is assigned to anything within quotation marks.

All variables are assigned by use of a LET statement, followed by the name of the variable, an equals sign, and then the value which is to be assigned to the variable.

CHAPTER 7
INPUT

The INPUT statement is used to get information from a user while a program is actually running. The computer stops when it comes to an INPUT statement and waits for an entry of some kind from the keyboard before it continues with the execution of the program.

Enter and run the following program, which shows numeric inputs in action. The program will wait for you to enter one number and then press ENTER, and then it will wait for another number. After you have pressed ENTER again, it will print the sum of the two numbers.

```
10  REM **INPUT**
20  INPUT X
30  PRINT ,X
40  INPUT Y
50  PRINT ,Y
60  LET Z=X+Y
70  PRINT ,"_____"
80  PRINT ,Z
90  PRINT ,"_____"
```

```
324
199
____
523
```

This is all right so far as it goes, but you would not have known what to do when you ran the program unless you had read it in this book. There is a simple way to rectify this by programming in user prompts. The preceding program can easily be rewritten so that the user has no doubt as to what he or she is meant to do.

```
10 REM **INPUT**
15 PRINT "GIVE ME A NUMBER"
20 INPUT X
30 PRINT ,X
35 PRINT "AND ANOTHER"
40 INPUT Y
50 PRINT ,Y
60 LET Z=X+Y
70 PRINT ,"     "
80 PRINT ,Z
90 PRINT ,"     "
```

```
GIVE ME A NUMBER
                    435
AND ANOTHER
                    288

                    723
```

Running this shows that the computer prints up the words within the quotation marks, then waits for the input.

Combat

Here's another program showing INPUT in action.

```
 5 REM **COMBAT**
10 LET SCORE=0
15 FOR J=1 TO 20
20 PRINT AT 0,0;"ENTER A NUMBE
R FROM 1 TO 10";AT 1,8;"GO NUMBE
R ";J
30 INPUT A
40 IF A<1 OR A>10 THEN GOTO 30
50 PRINT AT 10,0;"YOUR NUMBER
IS ";A;AT 12,6;"SCORE IS ";SCORE
60 FOR G=1 TO 4
70 LET B=INT (RND*10)+1
80 PRINT AT 3,3;B;" "
90 IF B=A THEN GOTO 110
100 NEXT G
110 IF A=B THEN LET SCORE=SCORE
+1
130 IF A=B THEN PRINT AT 14,8;"
WELL DONE"
```

```
 140  IF A<>B THEN PRINT AT 14,8;
"BAD LUCK"
 150  PRINT AT 12,6;"SCORE IS ";S
CORE
 160  IF SCORE=5 THEN GOTO 250
 170  FOR T=1 TO 20
 180  NEXT T
 190  CLS
 200  NEXT J
 210  PRINT "THE GAME IS OVER"
 220  PRINT "AND YOU ONLY SCORED
 ";SCORE
 230  PRINT "YOUR RATING IS ";SCO
RE/.05;" PERCENT"
 240  STOP
 250  PRINT "YOU DID IT"
 260  SCROLL
 270  PRINT "YOU WIN"
 280  GOTO 260
```

```
ENTER A NUMBER FROM 1 TO 10
        GO NUMBER 9

    10

YOUR NUMBER IS 6

     SCORE IS 3

     BAD LUCK
```

In COMBAT, you select a number between 1 and 10. The computer selects up to four numbers between 1 and 10. For each number that is the same as yours your score is increased by one. If you get a score of five within your 20 tries, you win. If not, you fail and get a percentage rating. Once you've run the program, come back to the book to go through it line by line. Although the program is fairly trivial, running it, then reading the explanatior will increase your knowledge of several aspects of BASIC.

5	Title.
10	Sets the variable SCORE to zero.
15	Starts the master FOR/NEXT loop to count your goes.
20	Asks the player to enter a number.
30	Accepts the input for variable A.
40	Checks that the input is legal.

50	Prints out the number chosen and the score. Note that PRINT statements may be *chained* in this way, with semicolons and the use of AT or TAB.
60–100	Generates up to four numbers. After each number is generated (line 70), it is printed (line 80) and checked against the player's number (line 90).
110	Score is increased by one if the guess is correct.
130	Prints WELL DONE if the guess is correct.
140	Prints BAD LUCK if the guess is incorrect.
150	Reprints the score.
170–180	Short delay before next move.
190	Clears the screen.
200	The end of the master FOR/NEXT loop.
210–240	End of game, if you lose.
250	End of game, if you win.

Compound interest

This next program will show the INPUT statement in action again and the use of explicit names for variables, which will make it easier to understand what is going on. You may want to save this program on cassette, as it has a degree of practical application.

YEAR	SIMPLE	COMPOUND	DIFF.
1	108.25	108.25	0
2	116.5	117.18	0.68
3	124.75	126.84	2.09
4	133	137.31	4.31
5	141.25	148.64	7.39
6	149.5	160.9	11.4
7	157.75	174.17	16.42
8	166	188.54	22.54
9	174.25	204.1	29.85
10	182.5	220.94	38.44
11	190.75	239.17	48.42
12	199	258.9	59.9

```
10 REM SIMPLE AND COMPOUND
20 REM        INTEREST
30 PRINT "PRINCIPAL?"
40 INPUT PRINCIPAL
45 PRINT "INTEREST?"
50 INPUT INTEREST
```

```
 55 PRINT "FOR HOW MANY YEARS?"
 60 INPUT YEARS
 70 CLS
 80 SCROLL
 90 PRINT "YEAR";TAB 6;"SIMPLE"
;TAB 15;"COMPOUND";TAB 25;"DIFF.
"
 95 SCROLL
100 PRINT "▞▚▞▚▞▚▞▚▞▚▞▚▞▚▞▚▞▚▞▚
▞▚▞▚▞▚▞▚▞"
110 FOR M=1 TO YEARS
120 LET SIMPLE=PRINCIPAL+M*PRIN
CIPAL*(INTEREST/100)
125 LET SIMPLE=INT (SIMPLE*100)
/100
130 LET COMPOUND=INT (100*PRINC
IPAL*(1+INTEREST/100)**M)/100
135 IF M=1 THEN LET COMPOUND=SI
MPLE
140 LET DIFF=INT (100*(COMPOUND
-SIMPLE+.005))/100
150 SCROLL
160 PRINT M;TAB 6;SIMPLE;TAB 15
;COMPOUND;TAB 25;DIFF
170 NEXT M
```

This program works out compound and simple interest, for a principal and interest rate you determine, over the number of years you decide. The example uses a principal of $100, at 8.25 percent over 12 years.

To stop a program during a string INPUT (BREAK does not operate during INPUTs), use cursor left (shift 5) or RUBOUT (shift Ø) to get the cursor out of the quotes, then type in STOP (shift A) followed by ENTER. If you are in a numeric INPUT without quotes, just type STOP (shift A) followed by ENTER. In both cases the program stops with report D. It is useful to be able to reject invalid inputs *before* they cause a program to crash.

If you invite a user to have another go and analyze his or her reply as follows:

```
555 PRINT "DO YOU WANT ANOTHER
GO?"
556 INPUT R$
557 IF R$="Y" THEN RUN
```

there is a law somewhere that says the user will respond by pressing only ENTER, leaving you with a null INPUT. There's no such thing as R$ (1)—it does not exist, as the computer will very quickly tell you in the form of an error report!

Here is one method of preventing this:

```
550 DIM R$(1)
555 PRINT "DO YOU WANT ANOTHER
GO?"
556 INPUT R$
557 IF R$(1)="Y" THEN RUN
```

Because R$ has previously been DIMensioned, it will have to consist of one character, no matter what is entered. If only ENTER is pressed, then R$ will be a space since that is what is placed in R$ after DIM and a null INPUT will not change it. If the INPUT is several characters long, then there is only room in R$ for the first character. If this character is Y, then the program will RUN for another go. This method has the advantage that if the user enters a very long reply such as "YES PLEASE NICE KIND COMPUTER, I WOULD LIKE VERY MUCH TO HAVE ANOTHER GO AT YOUR GREAT GAME PROGRAM" (very unlikely!) there is no need to store it all in memory. It is also very useful if you GOTO or do nothing that would CLEAR the variables, thus storing the entire reply unnecessarily. The second method is more conventional and uses one program line less than the previous routine, although it does place the entire reply unnecessarily in memory:

```
555 PRINT "DO YOU WANT ANOTHER
GO?"
556 INPUT R$
557 IF CODE R$=CODE "Y" THEN RU
N
```

The program explains itself really. If the first character of the reply has a CODE that is the same as the CODE of Y (i.e., it *is* Y), then the program RUNs again. Null INPUTs are rejected, since they are interpreted as meaning that the user does not want to play again. Merely pressing ENTER gives the empty string and the CODE of the empty string as Ø like a space. Checking the first letter of a user's INPUT is fairly easy as you've just seen. It becomes a bit more difficult when you want to check an entire INPUT, e.g., to see if the user has entered any punctuation marks or has included letters in a numeric INPUT. Let us look at alphabetic INPUTs first. The relational operators $>$, $<$, $<=$, $>=$, $<>$ are very useful in this case. Take the case of an INPUT where a word is strictly required and nothing else must be entered.

```
10  INPUT A$
15  IF A$="" THEN GOTO 10
20  FOR A=1 TO LEN A$
30  IF A$(A)<"A" OR A$(A)>"Z" T
HEN GOTO 10
40  NEXT A
```

Line 15 ensures that null INPUTs (i.e., just ENTER pressed) are rejected. The loop starting at line 20 scans the entire INPUT string character by character, and if a character is found which is not a letter, you are instructed to enter the string once again because the program jumps back to line 10. As it stands, the program will not allow spaces between words.

Change line 30 like this to allow spaces:

```
30  IF (A$(A)<"A" OR A$(A)>"Z")
AND A$(A)<>" " THEN GOTO 10
```

You can easily extend this idea to allow punctuation marks, letters, and spaces if you like (i.e., numbers, keywords, symbols, etc. are not allowed) by extending the idea in line 30. Only slightly more difficult is detecting a given word in an INPUT; e.g., if you wanted to have a line at the tail end of a program inviting the user to have another go at the program, so that if the user replied "YES", then the program would run again. It is a fairly simple thing to put the INPUT in a loop and slide the word along like this:

```
7000  PRINT "ANOTHER GO?"
7010  INPUT A$
7020  FOR A=1 TO LEN A$-2
7030  IF A$(A TO A+2)="YES" THEN
RUN
7040  NEXT A
7050  STOP
```

If you entered "YES" or "YES PLEASE" the program will rerun as required. If a word with a length that is less than the length of the search word is INPUTed (except the empty string), then this will cause an error because of line 7030 which expects the INPUT to be at least equal to the search word. The empty string is all right because then LEN A$ is 0, making line 7020 FOR A=1 TO -2, so the string is totally bypassed and the problem does not arise. Try also entering

"YESTERDAY"—the routine reruns because it has detected the three letters "YES". What is needed is a routine that detects if the character on either side of those three letters is anything other than a letter. We need to be careful doing this because we cannot examine the characters before and after the three letters "YES" if they occur at the beginning or at the end of an INPUT; they do not exist, and to attempt to examine them would cause a subscript error. Here is a routine which makes allowances for this by adding dummy characters at the start and end of A$.

```
7000 PRINT "ANOTHER GO?"
7010 INPUT A$
7015 LET A$=" "+A$+" "
7020 FOR A=2 TO LEN A$-3
7030 IF A$(A TO A+2)="YES" AND (
A$(A-1)<"A" OR A$(A-1)>"Z") AND
(A$(A+3)<"A" OR A$(A+3)>"Z") THE
N RUN
7040 NEXT A
7050 STOP
```

The routine takes about 180 bytes of memory, and allows all lengths of INPUT up to the maximum length that a string may be. If you want to change the search word in a program, then it may be worth assigning it to a variable or having an INPUT somewhere in the program for the search word. You will have to make the following modifications to the routine to use a different search word:

```
7000 PRINT "ENTER SEARCH WORD"
7010 INPUT S$
7020 PRINT "ENTER SENTENCE"
7030 INPUT A$
7040 LET A$=" "+A$+" "
7050 LET LS=LEN S$
7060 LET LA=LEN A$
7070 FOR A=2 TO LA-LS
7080 IF A$(A TO A+LS-1)=S$ AND (
A$(A-1)<"A" OR A$(A-1)>"Z") AND
(A$(A+LS)<"A" OR A$(A+LS)>"Z") T
HEN RUN
7090 NEXT A
7100 STOP
```

If the routine is a bit too long, then, provided you are using the same search word every time, you can avoid using S$ and LS and spell out the search word in full every time it is used, and replace all references to LS with the length of the search word. See the example using "YES" above.

The words AND and OR have been used several times in the past examples, so it is important that we know what they mean in a computer context.

The computer is constantly looking for information with which to make a TRUE or FALSE decision. If you say to it, in effect, "only if A is true *and* B is true then do something" the computer will check both conditions before doing whatever it is you have commanded. This is shown by the next program, which only prints the word YES if A is equal to 1 and B is equal to 1.

When you run it the first time, enter 1 for A and 1 for B, and you'll see it will print YES. Then try it with other numbers for B, to show that when AND is in the program line, the computer seeks to satisfy both conditions before acting. Here is the program:

```
10 PRINT "ENTER A NUMBER"
20 INPUT A
30 PRINT "YOUR FIRST NUMBER WA
S ";A
40 PRINT
50 PRINT "ENTER A SECOND NUMBE
R"
60 INPUT B
70 PRINT "YOUR SECOND NUMBER W
AS ";B
80 PRINT
90 IF A=1 AND B=1 THEN PRINT "
YES"
```

Now change line 90 so that the word AND becomes OR, and run it several times. You'll see that if either A *or* B is equal to 1, the computer will print YES. In summary, with AND both linked statements must be true; with OR the computer will act if it finds either one of them to be true.

Let us now look at another type of INPUT that is commonly used in games, both grid-type games and board games. This is an INPUT involving coordinates as you would find on some maps. For instance, you might have a board laid out like this:

	1	2	3	4	5
A					
B					
C					
D					
E					

The coordinates are usually entered in the form of a letter followed by a number, e.g., C3 if you are referring to one square as in a game such as "hunt the hurkle" or C3B4 if you are using from-to coordinates in a board game such as checkers. If you have decided that the coordinates are to be entered in the form of a letter followed by a number, chances are that sooner or later someone will—whether deliberately or accidentally—enter the coordinates in the wrong order and foul up the program. This routine will automatically detect if the two characters of a coordinate have been entered in the wrong order and sort them out. It applies to the board layout above; to modify it for other ranges of characters simply change the characters in quotes in lines 30 and 40. Line 50 has merely been included so that you can see the effect of the routine if any.

```
10  INPUT A$
20  IF LEN A$<2 THEN GOTO 10
25  LET A$=A$( TO 2)
30  IF A$(1)>="1" AND A$(1)<="5
" AND A$(2)>="A" AND A$(2)<="E"
THEN LET A$=A$(2)+A$(1)
```

```
40 IF A$(1)<"A" OR A$(1)>"E" O
R A$(2)<"1" OR A$(2)>"5" THEN GO
TO 10
50 PRINT A$
```

The routine takes about 245 bytes and is very quick to run. It is a very difficult routine to crash, but I'm sure some clever reader will find a way. If you do find a way of beating the routine, then modify the routine to prevent that error happening again.

The routine for a four-character coordinate is somewhat more complex. The idea of this INPUT is that you can enter the number of the square you are moving *from* and the square you are moving *to* in one go; e.g., E3D4 would mean that you moved a piece from square E3 to square D4. Let us first arrange the letters and numbers into order.

```
10 INPUT A$
20 IF LEN A$<4 THEN GOTO 10
30 LET A$=A$( TO 4)
40 IF A$(1)>="1" AND A$(1)<="5
" AND A$(2)>="A" AND A$(2)<="E"
THEN LET A$( TO 2)=A$(2)+A$(1)
50 IF A$(3)>="1" AND A$(3)<="5
" AND A$(4)>="A" AND A$(4)<="E"
THEN LET A$(3 TO )=A$(4)+A$(3)
60 IF A$(1)<"A" OR A$(1)>"E" O
R A$(2)<"1" OR A$(2)>"5" OR A$(3
)<"A" OR A$(3)>"E" OR A$(4)<"1"
OR A$(4)>"5" THEN GOTO 10
70 PRINT A$
```

Note that you can shorten these two routines by using the DIM command. In the first program you can add

```
5 DIM A$(2)
```

and delete lines 20 and 25. For the second program add

```
5 DIM A$(4)
```

and delete lines 20 and 30. What both versions achieve is to ensure that string A$ is neither shorter nor longer than the required length. If you enter an INPUT which is longer than four characters in the second routine, then the rest of the characters are ignored. If the number of characters entered is less than four characters, spaces are added if you have added line 5 to your program (then rejected in line 60) or rejected in line 2Ø if you are using the unmodified version. Having sorted out the letters and numbers, let us look at sorting out legal and illegal moves. You will need to look at the sample board shown earlier for this. Suppose we have an uncrowned checkers piece on square E3. We need to work out the legal moves from there. An uncrowned checkers piece can only move one square forward in a diagonal direction. The squares it may end up on are D2 or D4. Before reading on, can you work out the relationship between the coordinates?

Since the piece can only move forward one square at a time, it has to end up on a square whose letter is alphabetically nearest to E. Now, on your computer, the CODEs of letters that follow each other alphabetically step up or down by 1, so that the CODE of D is 1 less than the CODE of E. Therefore, if the CODE of the *from* square letter is not 1 greater than the CODE of the *to* square letter, then it is not a legal move. The number of the *from* square must be 1 greater or 1 less than the number of the *to* square, so we end up with:

```
65 IF NOT (CODE A$(1)=CODE A$(
3)+1) OR NOT ((CODE A$(2)=CODE A
$(4)+1) OR (CODE A$(2)=CODE A$(4
)-1)) THEN GOTO 10
```

Obviously you will need to adapt these routines to suit your programs, and they are only intended to show you the basis of routines that you may like to incorporate into your programs. They also help to demonstrate the approach you need to take to solve problems of this kind. For what it's worth, we suggest you try to follow these guidelines:

1. Work out exactly what you want to accomplish.
2. Work out exactly what is permitted, and some of the things which are not allowed (e.g., the empty string).
3. Figure out how you can prevent these happening, or reject them when they do happen.
4. Quickly work out in your head whether your routine does what you think it will by using it with a couple of examples.
5. If you are happy with your routine, enter it into the computer and try it out with some permitted values or characters to check whether there is a bug that prevents these values being entered. When happy with this, try

out the routine with all sorts of INPUTs (for example, try entering a nonexistent coordinate such as F9 in the routines above). You are now ready for the most important test.

6. Let a friend loose on the routine with orders to make a fool of the routine. The above routines do have a fallacy but I'm not telling you what it is; that's an exercise for you.

Finally, let's look at numeric INPUTs. Clear the computer with NEW and enter the following:

```
10 INPUT A
20 GOTO 10
```

RUN this little program and see if you can cause it to crash in any way; it shouldn't be too difficult. Try entering a letter; try entering STOP; try entering a number too large or too small for the computer to handle; or try entering a keyword or arithmetic sign such as +.

Arithmetic signs cause the computer to display a syntax error marker, although it does not stop the program. Keywords and symbols also cause this to happen, although letters cause the program to stop with error code 2, which means that an undefined variable has been used. Variable? Yes. When you enter a letter in response to a numeric INPUT, the computer thinks you're entering a variable and this can sometimes be very useful. With the same program, enter 1 on the first INPUT, then enter A the second time, and it is accepted! What the computer has done is look up the value of A and assigned it to A—in other words it hasn't changed the value of A. Now enter STOP. The program stops with error D. Now try typing in PRINT A, and you get the number 1, so the program has stopped *before* updating the value of A. In fact if you do manage to crash a numeric INPUT then in general the computer retains the previous value of the variable. Not that it's all that useful, but under certain circumstances if you do manage to restart the program, then the variable does have a value.

The easiest way to get around these problems is to use string INPUTs and evaluate using VAL. Try:

```
10 INPUT A$
20 LET A=VAL A$
30 PRINT A
40 GOTO 10
```

You should find this quite easy to crash, and many things true of numeric INPUTs seem to happen with this little routine. However, the advantage of this method is that it does not crash until you apply VAL if there is an error. You can process the string before applying VAL after INPUTing it and spot or remove errors before they crash—that is, you can *process* the string. The thing to remember is that VAL can work with anything numeric, not just numbers. Try the following:

```
PRINT VAL "RND"
PRINT VAL "SGN -7"
PRINT VAL "A*2"
PRINT VAL "COS 1"
```

(This only works if you have previously defined A, of course.)

Undefined variable names are the curse of VAL, along with nonnumeric statements or keywords or symbols. These have to be weeded out before you can apply VAL. The easiest case is that where only numeric INPUTs are allowed and you can do that like this:

```
10 INPUT A$
20 FOR F=1 TO LEN A$
30 IF A$(F)<"0" OR A$(F)>"9" T
HEN GOTO 10
40 NEXT F
50 LET A=VAL A$
60 PRINT A
```

Can you see straight away what would defeat the routine? Our old friend the empty string, of course. This would bypass the loop FOR F = 1 TO Ø, making it totally useless; so you have to add 15 IF A$ = " " THEN GOTO 1Ø. The routine makes you enter the number again if you have entered anything but numbers. You can extend the idea to permit arithmetic symbols and variable names if you like, but there is so little use for this that it hardly seems worthwhile:

```
30 IF (A$(F)<"0" OR A$(F)>"9")
AND (A$(F)<>"+" AND A$(F)<>" ")
THEN GOTO 10
```

This allows you to enter addition symbols and exponentiation symbols. To permit additional functions, simply add them within the second set of brackets linked together by AND. This is not terribly useful, but you may find a use for it someday.

We'll be looking at VAL and other string-processing functions in detail a little later in the book, but for now, we need to examine commands which lie at the heart of the computer's power to "think."

CHAPTER 8
Conditional statements

IF/THEN GOTO

The IF statement has a similar function to GOTO, but it will only reroute the program IF certain conditions are fulfilled. This creates a *conditional branch*. The IF/THEN statement is made up of a line number followed by the words IF/THEN GOTO separated by a relationship which must be determined before leaving the line. There are six relation operators which can be used to compare two variables. These are:

=   equal to
>   greater than
<   less than
< >   not equal to
>=   greater than or equal to
<=   less than or equal to

These operators are used to connect the IF/THEN statements to form the condition to be determined.

Here's an example: 70 IF Z >= 10 THEN GOTO 100.

This will be read by the computer to mean IF the value of the variable Z is greater than, or equal to, 10 THEN the program will branch to line 100. If Z is less than 10, the program will continue normal execution, with line 80. This gives the computer decision-making power, the real source of a computer's apparent ability to think.

As you've probably discovered, the computer isn't indecisive (unless you tell it to be); it makes a firm decision every time whether or not to do something. What it actually does depends on what you tell it to do, usually after the word

THEN in the line. Let's illustrate this with a simple program to print out the number you have just entered in words instead of digits.

```
10 PRINT "ENTER A NUMBER 1 TO
3"
20 INPUT A
30 IF A=1 THEN PRINT "ONE"
40 IF A=2 THEN PRINT "TWO"
50 IF A=3 THEN PRINT "THREE"
```

You need not be limited to one condition between the IF and THEN. To take the example above, suppose you were allowed to go home at five o'clock only if you'd finished your work; i.e., IF it's five o'clock AND you've finished your work THEN go home. When you want to join two or more conditional expressions such as "you've finished your work," you can use three connecting words to join the expressions. These are AND, OR, and NOT. If you have a conditional expression with AND joining the two parts, then the computer only does something if both parts are true. For example, if it's five o'clock but you haven't finished your work, then you are not entitled to go home.

To illustrate TRUE and FALSE, try this program:

```
10 INPUT A
20 INPUT B
30 IF A=1 AND B=1 THEN PRINT "
TRUE"
```

Try entering different values and see the results. Try changing the values in line 30 to see what effect this has. Make a note of your answers until you understand what's going on.

Let's look at OR. Think of OR along the lines of IF it's five o'clock OR the boss says you can leave early THEN go home, that is, do something when one of the alternatives is true. More correctly, do something when at least one of the alternatives is true, because it does not matter how many are true (they may all be) as long as at least one is true. So you go home at five o'clock anyway, but you may also go home when the boss says you may—either fact entitles you to go home. Try experimenting with this program in the same way as you experimented with the previous program.

```
10 INPUT A
20 INPUT B
30 IF A=1 OR B=1 THEN PRINT "T
RUE"
```

The last word (they're actually called *logical operations*) is NOT. It doesn't join expressions like the other two, but changes their meanings. Study this: If NOT the manager has said you can go home THEN stay at work. This means that unless you've been told that you may go home, you must stay at work. What happens is that the computer looks at the expression and decides that if it isn't true it will do something (for this purpose ignore the NOT for deciding what is true and what isn't). That is, IF NOT/THEN is true when whatever follows NOT is false. Something is done only when a condition is *not* met. Try this:

```
10 INPUT A
20 INPUT B
30 IF NOT A=B THEN PRINT "TRUE
"
```

This may confuse you at first, but if you experiment with the values of A and B, you will notice a pattern of results which illustrate the workings of NOT.

You may have noticed that we have used the = symbol in all the examples so far. Remember, this is only one of six *relational operators*. Refer to the list presented earlier of the six operators used on your computer.

Change the programs so that you use all of these relational operators. Play around with the programs until you find yourself able to predict what happens each time. Try combinations of AND, OR, and NOT and see in which order they are worked out. See if you can work out how to change the result by putting brackets around expressions. Note that this will not work in every case, so if a certain expression gives problems, leave it and try another one. This order of evaluation is called *priorities*, and is dealt with in detail later in this book.

We can apply conditional expressions to strings as well as numbers, e.g.:

```
10 INPUT A
20 INPUT B
30 LET X=(A=B)
40 PRINT X
```

RUN this program to see what happens. The first time you RUN it, enter the name FRED BLOGGS. The program comes to a halt normally. Pretty unexciting. RUN it again and this time try entering your own name (if your name happens to be FRED BLOGGS then enter somebody else's name). This time the program will self-destruct because of the NEW in line 20. If you substitute your name or a code number for FRED BLOGGS, then you will have a program that will only work for you or those that know the code, and will self-destruct if anyone else attempts to use it.

Let us now look at values in conditional expressions. First of all we'll use the relational operators. You will find that true is represented by 1 and false by 0.

```
10 INPUT A$
20 IF A$<>"FRED BLOGGS" THEN N
EW
```

The parentheses are not essential, but they do make it easier to understand what is happening. As the computer represents true by 1, and false by 0, replacing the second equals sign with any of the relational operators (that is, by a "greater than," a "less than," a "not equal," or whatever) will cause the program to give a 0 or a 1, depending on whether or not the particular statement is true.

The 0 and 1 results can be put to good use within a program. The best way to do this is to multiply some other value by the result of the true/false (that is, the 1 or 0 which results when you compare the two values) test. It means that true values will change, but false ones will not, as anything multiplied by 0 is 0.

Try changing the program to this:

```
10 INPUT A
20 INPUT B
30 LET X=(A=B) *2
40 PRINT X
```

This time you should get a value of 0 for a false expression and 2 for a true expression. The point of all this is that these values of conditional expressions are numbers and can be treated as numbers and this is very useful. Here is a simple game program, BLOB CATCHER, to illustrate the use of what we've just been discussing.

Note the double quotes in line 100. You get these from the Q key, holding down SHIFT. Do not try to enter it as the ordinary quotes (from the P key) twice. The quotes from the Q are useful when you wish to include quotes *within* a pair of quote marks in a PRINT statement. (By the way, the double quotes from the Q is called the *quote image*.)

```
 10 RAND
 20 LET S=0
 30 PRINT AT 9,9;"█ 1 2 3 4 5
";AT 5,8;"TIME:0  SCORE:0"
 40 FOR F=INT (RND*30)+10 TO 0
STEP -1
 50 LET A=INT (RND*5)+1
 60 PRINT AT 8,CODE "█£?>+"(A);
"█";AT 5,13;F;TAB 22;S
 65 IF F<10 THEN PRINT AT 5,14;
"█"
 70 LET S=S+(INKEY$=STR$ A)*A
 80 PRINT AT 8,CODE "█£?>+"(A);
" "
 90 NEXT F
100 PRINT AT 15,10;"THAT""S ALL
"
```

The idea of the game is to press the same key as the number under the moving blob; for instance, if the blob lands on 3 then you must press the 3 key, and you will score the number, and in this case 3 is added to your score. The number of attempts you have left is continuously displayed on screen as is your score. Line 70 is the one we're interested in at the moment. Here if STR$ A (the value of A converted to a string so that it can be compared with the key pressed) is the same as the key pressed, then the logical value is 1 because the expression is true. Whatever the value, it is multiplied by the value of A. If A is equal to 0, then the score does not change. If A is equal to 1, then the score changes by 1*A, or A. The score is counted by the variable S. The number of attempts left is counted by F.

Let us now move to look at values in conditional expressions involving the logical operations AND, OR, and NOT.

X AND Y has the value X if Y is true (nonzero) or 0 if Y is false (zero). X and Y can be expressions like X=2 or Y =2*B. One common application is to control on-screen movement. Many games use the cursor-arrow keys to control movement on screen. This is one way of moving an object left or right along the screen:

```
10 LET X=15
20 IF INKEY$="5" AND X>1 THEN
LET X=X-2
30 IF INKEY$="8" AND X<30 THEN
LET X=X+2
40 PRINT AT 21,X;"█";AT 21,X;"
"
50 GOTO 20
```

This moves a blob two columns at a time along the bottom row of the screen. You can do the same thing with:

```
10 LET X=15
20 LET X=X-(INKEY$="5" AND X>1
)*2+(INKEY$="8" AND X<30)*2
30 PRINT AT 21,X;"█";AT 21,X;"
"
40 GOTO 20
```

Or with:

```
10 LET X=15
20 LET X=X-(2 AND INKEY$="5" A
ND X>1)+(2 AND INKEY$="8" AND X<
30)
30 PRINT AT 21,X;"█";AT 21,X;"
"
40 GOTO 20
```

The point to note with the last two programs is that the expressions in brackets take the value of the number before the first AND if all the expressions after the AND are true. Compare these with X AND Y, which we have just discussed. Here X is a number (2 in this case) and not an expression. You can think of line 20 above as 20 LET X = X − (2 if the 5 key is pressed and if the value of X is greater than 1, otherwise 0) + (2 if the 8 key is pressed and the value of X is less than 30, otherwise 0).

You might think why go to these complications to do something that could be done equally well by a series of IF/THEN lines. The answer is that, used properly and in the right circumstances, several program lines can be replaced by one long conditional expression, thus saving memory and possibly making the program RUN faster. In addition, when you become more familiar with these conditional expressions, you will find that sometimes they can actually clarify listings over a long set of IF/THEN statements. AND can be applied to string variables and string constants as well, e.g.:

```
10 PRINT "ENTER YOUR NAME"
20 INPUT A$
30 LET A$=(A$ AND A$<>"FRED BL
OGGS")+("MASTER" AND A$="FRED BL
OGGS")
40 PRINT "HELLO ";A$
```

or you can replace 30 and 40 by

```
30 PRINT "HELLO ";(A$ AND A$<>
"FRED BLOGGS")+("MASTER" AND A$=
"FRED BLOGGS")
```

The expression in parentheses takes the form of the first expression before AND in the parentheses if the expressions after AND are true. If false, the empty or null string is obtained. What the program does is recognize FRED BLOGGS as being its master and acknowledges this by PRINTing MASTER. This could be circumvented if you wished by adding an extra space between FRED and BLOGGS when entering the name, to fool all concerned. This routine saves nothing over:

```
10 PRINT "ENTER YOUR NAME"
20 INPUT A$
30 IF A$="FRED BLOGGS" THEN LE
T A$="MASTER"
40 PRINT "HELLO ";A$
```

However, if you wanted to print out different messages for a list of names, then you can save a great deal of memory by using this method. Try writing a program that will in one line sort out which message to print for each of these names:

message	name
MASTER	FRED
IDIOT	JIM
TOM	TOM
BEAUTIFUL	JILL

Yes, it can be done! Here's how:

```
30 LET A$=("MASTER" AND A$="FR
ED")+("IDIOT" AND A$="JIM")+(A$
AND A$<>"FRED" AND A$<>"JIM" AND
A$<>"JILL")+("BEAUTIFUL" AND A$
="JILL")
```

If you had (A$ AND A$ = "TOM") instead of (A$ AND A$ <> "FRED" and A$ <> "JIM" and A$ <> "JILL") you were wrong—it would work for those four names but if any other name is entered, you get the null string which isn't very useful. You may have noticed that the examples mainly use addition or subtraction—this is because of the default value of zero not affecting the results in addition or subtraction. We shall see now that OR is used mainly for multiplication or division.

X OR Y has the value 1 if Y is nonzero (true) or X if Y is zero (false).

OR cannot be applied to strings as we saw with AND above. Let us take this example to illustrate the action of OR in this context: Suppose a conductor on a bus wanted a program to let him know what fare to charge a schoolchild, and that the age limit for these reduced fares was 14.

```
 5 PRINT "FARE?"
10 INPUT FARE
15 PRINT "AGE?"
20 INPUT AGE
30 LET FARE=FARE*(0.5 OR AGE>1
4)
40 PRINT FARE
```

Lines 10 and 20 ask you to enter the normal adult fare and the age of the passenger/commuter. Now then, to understand this a little better, let us convert it to plainer English: LET FARE = FARE*(0.5 unless his or her age is over 14). If the expression following OR in brackets is true, then the expression in brackets has the value 1. However, if the expression following OR is false (he or she is 14 or younger), then the expression takes the value before the OR. This number can also be a variable if you like. On its own this routine does not have much to offer against:

```
30 IF AGE<=14 THEN LET FARE=FA
RE*0.5
```

However, if you had several categories of fares on offer,

then the method using OR can be extended to evaluate all the categories on one line.

NOT X takes the value of 0 if the relation X is true and the value 1 if the relation is false. The best way to illustrate this is with this kind of example:

```
10 INPUT A
20 INPUT B
30 PRINT A;TAB 4;B;TAB 8;NOT (
A=B)
40 GOTO 10
```

What you will see on the screen are the two numbers you entered in lines 10 and 20, followed by a 0 or a 1. From the results you get, see if you can work out which relationships between A and B produce which values in the third column. Try other relational operators in place of = in line 30. Why do some relations produce the same results as others without NOT? Try changing line 30 to:

```
30 PRINT A;TAB 4;B;TAB 8;A<>B
```

Why does the program give the same results as the previous version above? Can you see similar results between other pairs of relations?

Finally, let us look at two interesting little oddities. First, consider this line:

```
10 IF A=1 THEN IF B=2 THEN PRI
NT "TRUE"
```

It's to all intents and purposes the same as

```
10 IF A=1 AND B=1 THEN PRINT "
TRUE"
```

except that it requires one extra byte in memory. There is a slight difference in that if you haven't previously defined B, the version using AND will crash with report 2. However, if the first part of the other version is false, the program skips over the remainder of the line. You may be able to find an application for this.

The second oddity is not really an oddity, more something that is missed by many people. Try these programs:

```
10 INPUT A
20 IF A THEN PRINT A
```

```
10 INPUT A
20 IF NOT A THEN PRINT A
```

You might not expect these programs to work because there are no relational operators for comparing A with anything. Here, however, the value of A is considered to be true if it is not 0, or 0 if you use NOT. As with everything else in this section, experiment with the examples until you understand exactly what each routine does. You will find that these statements can be very powerful programming facilities, and your programming can be greatly improved as a result.

You can use IF/THEN GOTO to terminate a "win condition" message after a certain number of cycles. Enter and run the following:

```
10 LET X=0
20 PRINT "YOU HAVE WON ";
30 LET X=X+1
40 IF X<25 THEN GOTO 20
```

This will ensure that YOU HAVE WON is printed out a limited number of times.

As you've seen, IF/THEN is not just used to branch to new lines. NEW the program, and enter the following. You'll see it has a similar effect, although the IF is not just sending the program to a line number.

```
10 LET X=0
20 LET X=X+1
30 IF X<25 THEN PRINT "YOU HAV
E WON ";
40 GOTO 20
```

This program is not as useful as the other one, as it will not stop even when it has finished printing out YOU HAVE WON. You can easily discover this by running it, then pressing BREAK, and then PRINT X, ENTER.

It is perhaps worth mentioning that the computer is a fairly dogmatic creature. If you specify that a program branch is to be made only if the value of Z, for example, is equal to 6, the program will continue in a never-ending loop if Z is not exactly equal to 6, no matter how close it is (like 5.999999). If you think the value might be fractionally different from the one you want as a condition for branching, make sure you specify that the relational operator should be, say, greater than 5.5, or greater than or equal to 5.9, rather than just equal to 6.

IF/THEN/ELSE

Many dialects of BASIC include an ELSE option, used in the statement IF/THEN/ELSE. There is no such function in our computer's BASIC, but its logic can be used to emulate this.

The IF/THEN/ELSE is a very useful variation on IF. The computer can be programmed to do something if the condition being tested for is found to be true, and something else, other than just go to the next line, if the condition is found to be false.

You can use the following substitution for IF/THEN/ELSE to produce some very interesting graphs in the next program. You simply enter the function you would like graphed in line 55. This is not the most efficient method of programming on the computers, but it is useful as a means of demonstrating the IF/THEN/ELSE substitution. As the program runs, it evaluates K each time it comes to line 55. Line 70 looks at the value of K and prints a 0 if K is greater than or equal to 0.5, and a period if K is less than 0.5. This is the same as a line reading IF K is greater than or equal to 0.5 THEN print "0" ELSE print ".". Each of the other graphs uses different values for K, as generated by line 55. The condition tested for in line 70 also varies. Run the samples given, using your own choice of graphics symbol in line 70, and then create a few of your own. It is likely that you'll have to change the scaling for certain functions.

```
10 REM GRAPH-PLOTTER
20 REM (C) W. J. FABERGE
30 FOR Y=10 TO -10 STEP -1
35 IF Y<>10 AND Y<>-10 AND Y>-
1 THEN PRINT " ";
40 PRINT Y;TAB 4;
50 FOR X=-10 TO 10
55 LET K=Y-X*X/2+7
70 PRINT ("0" AND K>=.5)+("."
AND K<.5);
110 NEXT X
120 PRINT
130 NEXT Y
140 PRINT TAB 4;".9.7.5.3.1.1.3
.5.7.9."
```

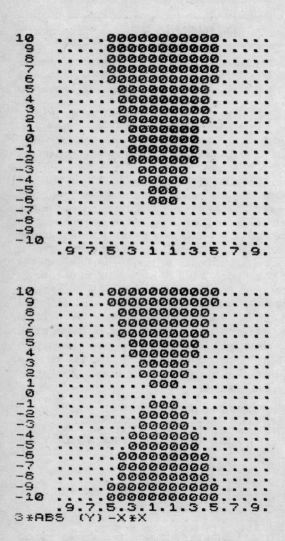

```
10    .....00000000000.....
 9    .....00000000000.....
 8    .....00000000000.....
 7    .....00000000000.....
 6    .....00000000000.....
 5    ......000000000......
 4    ......000000000......
 3    ......000000000......
 2    ......000000000......
 1    .......0000000.......
 0    .......0000000.......
-1    .......0000000.......
-2    .......0000000.......
-3    ........00000........
-4    ........00000........
-5    .........000.........
-6    .........000.........
-7    .....................
-8    .....................
-9    .....................
-10   .9.7.5.3.1.1.3.5.7.9.
```

```
10    .....00000000000.....
 9    .....00000000000.....
 8    ......000000000......
 7    ......000000000......
 6    ......000000000......
 5    .......0000000.......
 4    .......0000000.......
 3    ........00000........
 2    ........00000........
 1    .........000.........
 0    .....................
-1    .........000.........
-2    ........00000........
-3    ........00000........
-4    .......0000000.......
-5    .......0000000.......
-6    ......000000000......
-7    ......000000000......
-8    ......000000000......
-9    .....00000000000.....
-10   .....00000000000.....
      .9.7.5.3.1.1.3.5.7.9.
3*ABS (Y) -X*X
```

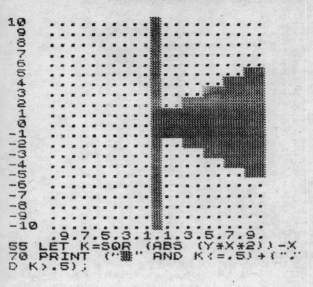

```
55 LET K=SQR (ABS (Y*X*2))-X
70 PRINT ("█" AND K<=.5)+("." AN
D K>.5);
```

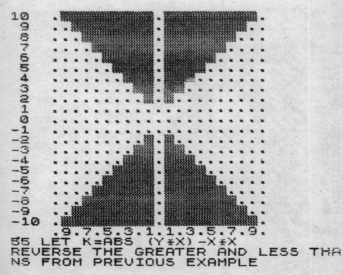

```
55 LET K=ABS (Y*X)-X*X
REVERSE THE GREATER AND LESS THA
NS FROM PREVIOUS EXAMPLE
```

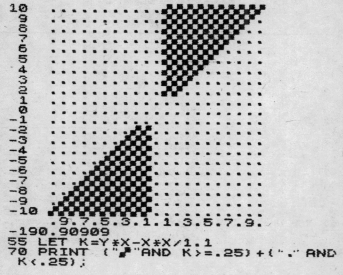

```
-190.90909
55 LET K=Y*X-X*X/1.1
70 PRINT ("█"AND K>=.25)+("."AND
K<.25);
```

Try to work out what line 55 should read to produce this graph:

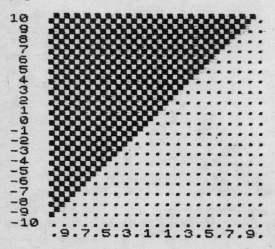

CHAPTER 9
Loops

FOR/NEXT loops

FOR/NEXT loops are additional useful parts of your BASIC working tools on the computer. It makes sense to study them now, because the last series of programs relied heavily on two FOR/NEXT loops, the Y loop which started at line 3Ø and ended at line 13Ø, and the X loop which ran from line 5Ø to line 11Ø. Because these are slightly more complex than the simplest FOR/NEXT loops, we'll leave the discussion of those alone for the time being.

A FOR/NEXT loop is controlled by two lines (one which reads something like FOR A = 1 TO 1000; the second, NEXT A). All the steps between these two lines are carried out once every time through the loop. The difference between the two numbers in the FOR statement, plus one (so in our example of FOR A = 1 TO 1000 the difference plus one would be 1000), is generally the number of times the steps between the lines are carried out.

For example, in the next program, the word TEST is printed out four times:

```
10 FOR A=1 TO 4
20 PRINT "TEST"
30 NEXT A

TEST
TEST
TEST
TEST
```

FOR statements are made up of the line number, followed by the FOR, a numeric variable (a single letter), an equals sign, a numeric expression (a number, or a previously assigned numeric variable), the word TO, and finally, another numeric expression (number of previously assigned numeric variable) which is different from the first one. That may sound incredibly complicated, but it is really quite simple.

The FOR line reads:

```
100 FOR J=1 TO 100
```

The NEXT line, which terminates the loop, is of the form:

```
200 NEXT J
```

The NEXT statement, then, is made up of a line number, the word NEXT, and the variable set as the control in the FOR statement, earlier in the program. The NEXT sequence is used solely to tell the computer when the sequence of programming which is being repeated is to stop. When the value of the control variable (J) reaches the value set in the FOR statement (the second numeric variable set in the FOR statement), the program passes through the loop for the final time and then continues with the line following the one containing the word NEXT.

Enter and run this example:

```
10 FOR A=1 TO 10
20 PRINT TAB 4;A;TAB 8;A*A
30 NEXT A
1    1
2    4
3    9
4    16
5    25
6    36
7    49
8    64
9    81
10   100
```

The control variable is A, and line 20 prints out A and A squared. Note that the limits of the control loop are stated explicitly in line 10 (1 TO 10).

Note that to avoid flicker when using PAUSE you can replace it with a FOR/NEXT loop (when running a program in the SLOW mode). For example, 10 PAUSE 500 could be replaced by:

```
10 FOR F=1 TO 500
20 NEXT F
```

A loop of 60 corresponds approximately to one second in practice as does PAUSE 60.

Look at this next example:

```
10 LET A=5
20 LET B=16
30 FOR C=A TO B
40 PRINT TAB 4;C;TAB 8;C/10;TA
B 14;C/A
50 NEXT C
```

```
5       0.5       1
6       0.6       1.2
7       0.7       1.4
8       0.8       1.6
9       0.9       1.8
10      1         2
11      1.1       2.2
12      1.2       2.4
13      1.3       2.6
14      1.4       2.8
15      1.5       3
16      1.6       3.2
```

Note that in this program the limits of the FOR/NEXT loop are two variables, A and B, which have been previously defined. You will find there are many programs where you will want a limited FOR/NEXT loop, with the limits a result of things that have occurred elsewhere in the program.

Nested loops

As you've just seen, a FOR/NEXT loop allows us to alter the value of one variable (by a count of one in the cases we've studied), to repeat a programmed series of events a specified number of times. Now, suppose there were two or more variables to be operated upon. In this case, you would need to vary both values. This can be done quite simply by *nesting* loops, in which one loop, controlled by one set of FOR/NEXT statements, operates within another set.

Enter and run the following program, which *nests* a B loop within an A loop:

```
10 REM NESTED LOOPS
20 FOR A=1 TO 12
30 FOR B=1 TO 12
40 SCROLL
50 PRINT TAB 8;B;" TIMES ";A;"
IS ";A*B
60 NEXT B
70 SCROLL
80 SCROLL
90 NEXT A
```

When you run this, you'll see it prints out the multiplication table, from 1×1 to 12×12. Part of the run is:

```
9 TIMES 7 IS 63
10 TIMES 7 IS 70
11 TIMES 7 IS 77
12 TIMES 7 IS 84

1 TIMES 8 IS 8
2 TIMES 8 IS 16
3 TIMES 8 IS 24
4 TIMES 8 IS 32
5 TIMES 8 IS 40
6 TIMES 8 IS 48
7 TIMES 8 IS 56
8 TIMES 8 IS 64
9 TIMES 8 IS 72
10 TIMES 8 IS 80
11 TIMES 8 IS 88
```

In this program, the control variable A stays at 1, while the loop controlled by B runs from 1 to 12. After the double scroll (lines 70 and 80), the control variable A increases by one, and the B loop runs through again, this time with the A equal to 2, and so on, until the B loop has run through with the A equal to 12. There is no reason why you should have only two nested loops.

It is vital that the control variables of nested loops be in the correct order, that is, that the first loop begun is the last one to end. Try swapping lines 60 and 90 of this program and see what happens.

This is part of the output:

```
1 TIMES 6 IS 6
1 TIMES 7 IS 7
1 TIMES 8 IS 8
1 TIMES 9 IS 9
1 TIMES 10 IS 10
1 TIMES 11 IS 11
1 TIMES 12 IS 12
```

```
2 TIMES 13 IS 26
3 TIMES 14 IS 42
4 TIMES 15 IS 60
5 TIMES 16 IS 80
```

Use the same variable for as many purposes as you can, especially when you use FOR/NEXT loops. Don't use another letter as the name for a second FOR/NEXT loop if you've already finished with a previous one, as this wastes working space memory consumed when the program is running. This may be important when you're running a program which is very close to using up all the available memory.

The following two sample programs show what I mean. The first uses less working space or memory than does the second, because it uses the same name (A) as the control variable in both loops. The second one, as you see, uses two different names (A and B).

```
10 FOR A=1 TO 4
20 PRINT A; " ";
30 NEXT A
40 FOR A=20 TO 25
50 PRINT A; " ";
60 NEXT A
```

```
10 FOR A=1 TO 4
20 PRINT A; " ";
30 NEXT A
40 FOR B=20 TO 25
50 PRINT B; " ";
60 NEXT B
```

STEP

For this next discussion, we need the program TABULATOR ROCKET RANGE. Enter and run the following program:

```
10 REM TABULATOR ROCKET RANGE
20 REM (C) CHARLTON 1982
25 DIM A$(5,5)
27 SCROLL
30 FOR J=10 TO 1 STEP -1
40 PRINT TAB 3*J; J
50 FOR A=1 TO J
52 SCROLL
55 NEXT A
```

```
70 NEXT J
71 LET A$(1)=" 🔲 "
72 LET A$(2)=" 🔲 "
73 LET A$(3)=" 🔲 "
74 LET A$(4)=" 🔲 "
75 LET A$(5)=" >*< "
80 REM ** MAIN PROGRAM **
90 LET Q=INT (RND*25)+1
110 FOR R=1 TO 5
115 SCROLL
120 PRINT "(";TAB (Q);A$(R);TAB
30;")"
130 NEXT R
170 LET SPACE=Q/3
180 FOR P=1 TO SPACE
185 SCROLL
190 PRINT "(";TAB 30;")"
200 NEXT P
210 GOTO 90
```

The important lines for our discussion at this point are 30, 40, and 70. You'll see when you run the program that this causes the numbers 10 down to 1 to appear on the screen. The word STEP (in line 30) after the 1 controls this. Change the -1 following the word STEP to -2, and see what happens. If no STEP is specified, the computer assumes you want a positive STEP of 1, which is what has been needed in the earlier examples in this section.

The STEP command, then, is used within a FOR/NEXT loop to allow the user to specify the value of the increment (or decrement) of the control variable. The STEP does not have to be a whole number, although you must ensure—if the number which follows the word TO in the initial FOR statement, the limit value, is lower than the number before the TO—that the STEP is negative. Try the following examples:

```
10 FOR A=100 TO 1 STEP -12.5
20 PRINT TAB 8;A
30 NEXT A

        100
        87.5
        75
        62.5
        50
        37.5
        25
        12.5
```

```
10 FOR A=10 TO 1 STEP -0.719
20 PRINT TAB 8;A
30 NEXT A

        10
        9.281
        8.562
        7.843
        7.124
        6.405
        5.686
        4.967
        4.248
        3.529
        2.81
        2.091
        1.372
```

In a FOR/NEXT loop, STEP does not have to be a whole number; it may be a fraction, a decimal, or the result of a calculation, and it does not have to hit the limit value of the loop exactly. It carries on looping as long as it is less than or equal to the limit. You cannot easily change the value of STEP during the course of a loop.

If the limit value has already been exceeded then loop will be totally bypassed, e.g.:

```
10 FOR I=1 TO 0
20 PRINT "X"
30 NEXT I
40 PRINT "Y"
```

You may be able to use this idea to prevent loops from being executed if certain conditions exist. For example, if you didn't want a black line to be drawn if X was equal to 6, you could have a program as follows. Note that X has to be entered at first, in line 10. Run it a few times, entering numbers other than 6, and see what happens, and then enter a 6.

```
10 INPUT X
20 PRINT "YOUR NUMBER WAS ";X
30 FOR A=(X=6)*32 TO 31
40 PRINT CHR$ 128;
50 NEXT A
60 GOTO 10
```

The test to see if the limit value has been exceeded is made at the line containing the FOR statement.

You might like to try a STEP value of 0. The control variable is never incremented, so the loop never ends. You can jump out of FOR/NEXT loops without any problems, but you cannot jump into a loop unless the control variable has already been set up (effectively if you've used that loop before). The loop jumps from NEXT to the line following the FOR statement in a FOR/NEXT loop.

CHAPTER 10
GOSUB and RETURN

A subroutine is a block of program within a larger program which performs one specific task. The main program is executed, line by line, until the subroutine is called, by the GOSUB command. The computer goes to the specified number, and works through in line order from that point until it hits the word RETURN. This is the signal for the computer to return to the main program, to the line *after* the one which sent it to the subroutine.

A subroutine is useful if a particular set of calculations has to be carried out a number of times within a program, and at different places within the program. For example, in a financial program, there may be a number of tax calculations to be carried out at different points within the program. Whenever this need arises, the program is told to GOSUB, and it stays in this subroutine until it hits the word RETURN, when it returns to the line *after* the GOSUB command.

A subroutine is written exactly like the main program, except that it is a program within a program, and is bounded by two lines, one containing the GOSUB and the other the RETURN line. The GOSUB command is made up from a line number, followed by the word GOSUB, and another line number. A line such as 40 GOSUB 100 tells the computer to branch to line 100 and continue executing the program in order, just as if line 40 had said GOTO 100. However, when the program reaches a line containing the word RETURN, the action reverts to the main program, at the line number which follows the one containing the GOSUB statement (in this case, the first line number after 40).

A simple example, showing GOSUB and RETURN, is as follows. Enter and run it a few times, then come back to the book for a discussion on it.

```
ENTER A NUMBER
YOUR NUMBER IS 24
24 SQUARED IS 576

ENTER A NUMBER
YOUR NUMBER IS 7
7 SQUARED IS 49

ENTER A NUMBER
YOUR NUMBER IS 888888
888888 SQUARED IS 790121580000

ENTER A NUMBER
YOUR NUMBER IS 87
87 SQUARED IS 7569
```

```
10 REM GOSUB/RETURN DEMO
20 SCROLL
30 PRINT "ENTER A NUMBER"
40 INPUT A
50 GOSUB 100
60 GOTO 20
90 REM SUBROUTINE FOLLOWS
100 SCROLL
110 PRINT "YOUR NUMBER IS ";A
120 SCROLL
130 PRINT A;" SQUARED IS ";A*A
140 SCROLL
150 RETURN
```

After line 20 SCROLLS the screen, line 40 asks you to
enter a number, and then line 50 transfers control to the
subroutine starting at line 100. The required calculations are
carried out, and the results of them printed, within the subroutine; then line 150 returns control to the line *after* the one
which sent control to the subroutine, that is, line 60. As line
60 is a GOTO, action goes back to line 20, where a new
number is requested, and the whole merry dance begins
again.

Enter and run the following program, which pits two submarines against each other in a race, to see a subroutine doing
something a little more interesting than in the preceding
program.

The graphics characters used in line 20 are from the 5 key,
then 29 spaces, followed by the graphics from the 6 key, the
Q, the space (so you get a solid square), and finally the
graphics from the 4 key.

```
 10 REM GOSUB RACE
 20 LET A$="▮    "
 30 LET COMPUTER=28
 40 LET HUMAN=28
 50 LET X=5
 60 GOSUB 100
 70 LET X=10
 80 GOSUB 100
 90 GOTO 50
100 IF X=5 THEN LET COMPUTER=CO
MPUTER-RND
110 IF X=10 THEN LET HUMAN=HUMA
N-RND
120 IF X=5 THEN PRINT AT X,COMP
UTER;A$
130 IF X=10 THEN PRINT AT X,HUM
AN;A$
140 IF X=5 AND COMPUTER<2 THEN
PRINT AT 0,0;"COMPUTER WINS";Q
150 IF X=10 AND HUMAN<2 THEN PR
INT AT 0,0;"HUMAN WINS";Q
160 RETURN
```

There are two "submarines" on the screen. The top one is the computer's, and the bottom one belongs to you. You just press RUN, then ENTER, and the submarines move across the screen from right to left. When one or the other reaches the side, the program stops, printing out COMPUTER WINS or HUMAN WINS, as the case may be. Notice the Q at the ends of lines 140 and 150. The computer stops when it reaches that (giving an error code 2), because the Q is an undefined variable. Using an undefined variable to stop a program in this way saves space. Without it, another two lines of the type IF X = 5 AND COMPUTER < 2 THEN STOP would be required. Note also that A$, the submarine, extends over more than one line. Just keep pressing SPACE over and over again once you've put in the "periscope" part of the picture. Note also that there is a space *after* the end of the submarine. This is vital, as you'll discover if you leave it out.

CHAPTER 11
DIM and arrays

The DIM command can be hard to understand, but taking the trouble to do so will be well repaid.

DIM tells the computer to reserve a certain number of spaces in its memory, to be filled later. A DIM command is followed by a letter (A to Z), then a number in parentheses. The number tells the computer how many spaces to reserve. For example, DIM A(20) tells the computer to set up a series of 20 spaces, which can be used as A(1), A(2), and so on. This list is called an *array,* and each part of the array, the A(1), A(2), and so on, is called an *element* of the array.

Enter and run the following program which should make it a little easier to understand:

```
10 REM **ARRAYS DEMO**
20 DIM B(4)
30 FOR A=1 TO 4
40 LET B(A)=INT (RND*9)+1
50 NEXT A
60 FOR A=1 TO 4
70 PRINT TAB 6;"B(";A;") IS ";
B(A)
80 NEXT A
```

```
B(1)  IS  6
B(2)  IS  6
B(3)  IS  7
B(4)  IS  5
```

As you can see from line 20 of the program you've just run, the computer needs you to DIMension an array with a DIM statement before you can use it. The DIM statement is made up of a line number followed by the word DIM, and the name of the array in the form of a letter, with the size of the array enclosed in parentheses.

70

The arrays we've been talking about so far are one-dimensional arrays, suitable for such things as holding a list of numbers. However, you can have arrays of more than one dimension. These arrays are called, reasonably enough, multidimensional arrays, and are set up with a DIM command having more than one subscript. Enter and run the following program:

```
 10 REM  MULTI-DIMENSIONAL
 20 REM         ARRAYS
 30 DIM A(4,4)
 40 FOR B=1 TO 4
 50 FOR C=1 TO 4
 60 LET A(B,C)=INT (RND*9)+1
 70 PRINT "A(";B;",";C;") IS ";
A(B,C)
 80 NEXT C
 90 NEXT B
100 PRINT AT 6,15;"1 2 3 4"
105 PRINT
110 FOR B=1 TO 4
120 PRINT TAB 13;B;TAB 15;A(B,1
);" ";A(B,2);" ";A(B,3);" ";A(B,
4)
130 NEXT B
```

When you run it you'll see something like this:

```
A(1,1)  IS  1
A(1,2)  IS  9
A(1,3)  IS  8
A(1,4)  IS  9
A(2,1)  IS  8
A(2,2)  IS  7
A(2,3)  IS  4          1 2 3 4
A(2,4)  IS  3
A(3,1)  IS  3       1  1 9 8 9
A(3,2)  IS  4       2  8 7 4 3
A(3,3)  IS  6       3  3 4 6 9
A(3,4)  IS  9       4  8 2 8 7
A(4,1)  IS  8
A(4,2)  IS  2
A(4,3)  IS  8
A(4,4)  IS  7
```

First, the elements of the array will be filled with numbers between 1 and 9, and these are printed out by line 70 so you can see what is held by each element of the array. The small table printed beside them shows how the elements of the array are organized. Any element can be accessed by giving its coordinates within the array. If this is so, element 3,3 should lie where the two threes intersect, i.e., on the number 6. You'll see from looking above in our sample run that, in fact, A(3,3) does equal 6.

DIMensioning an array consumes memory, so do not set up an array larger than you need. The number of elements in an array is the first number within the parentheses, multiplied by the second number. Therefore, the array A(4,4) has 16(4 × 4) elements. You can see from our sample run that this is so.

There is no reason why you should not have arrays with more than two dimensions, except for the fact that they can quickly become quite difficult to handle, and the number of elements rockets quite alarmingly. Here is a program to DIMension and fill a three-dimensional array. Although the array is only A(3,3,3), you can see that the number of elements is quite large (3*3*3).

```
10 REM MULTI-DIMENSIONAL
20 REM          ARRAYS
30 DIM A(3,3,3)
40 FOR B=1 TO 3
50 FOR C=1 TO 3
60 FOR D=1 TO 3
70 LET A(B,C,D)=INT (RND*9)+1
75 SCROLL
80 PRINT "A(";B;",";C;",";D;
90 PRINT ") IS ";A(B,C,D)
100 NEXT D
110 NEXT C
120 NEXT B
```

```
A(1,2,3)  IS  5
A(1,3,1)  IS  7
A(1,3,2)  IS  7
A(1,3,3)  IS  6
A(2,1,1)  IS  2
A(2,1,2)  IS  9
A(2,1,3)  IS  8
A(2,2,1)  IS  5
A(2,2,2)  IS  3
A(2,2,3)  IS  3
A(2,3,1)  IS  5
A(2,3,2)  IS  7
A(2,3,3)  IS  8
A(3,1,1)  IS  9
A(3,1,2)  IS  2
A(3,1,3)  IS  2
A(3,2,1)  IS  5
A(3,2,2)  IS  6
```

```
A(3,2,3)  IS  5
A(3,3,1)  IS  8
A(3,3,2)  IS  4
A(3,3,3)  IS  2
```

Increase the number of dimensions to five, as in our next example, and although it is only A(2,2,2,2,2), there are now 32 (2*2*2*2*2) elements.

```
10  REM  MULTI-DIMENSIONAL
20  REM        ARRAYS
30  DIM A(2,2,2,2,2)
40  FOR B=1 TO 2
50  FOR C=1 TO 2
60  FOR D=1 TO 2
70  FOR E=1 TO 2
80  FOR F=1 TO 2
90  LET A(B,C,D,E,F)=INT (RND*9
)+1
100  SCROLL
110  PRINT "A(";B;",";C;",";D;",
";E;",";F;
120  PRINT ") IS ";A(B,C,D,E,F)
130  NEXT F
140  NEXT E
150  NEXT D
160  NEXT C
170  NEXT B
```

```
A(1,2,1,2,1)  IS  6
A(1,2,1,2,2)  IS  8
A(1,2,2,1,1)  IS  5
A(1,2,2,1,2)  IS  5
A(1,2,2,2,1)  IS  9
A(1,2,2,2,2)  IS  9
A(2,1,1,1,2)  IS  9
A(2,1,1,1,2)  IS  9
A(2,1,1,2,1)  IS  2
A(2,1,1,2,2)  IS  3
A(2,1,2,1,1)  IS  1
A(2,1,2,1,2)  IS  6
A(2,1,2,2,1)  IS  8
A(2,1,2,2,2)  IS  9
A(2,2,1,1,1)  IS  4
A(2,2,1,1,2)  IS  7
A(2,2,1,2,1)  IS  2
A(2,2,1,2,2)  IS  2
A(2,2,2,1,1)  IS  9
A(2,2,2,1,2)  IS  9
A(2,2,2,2,1)  IS  9
A(2,2,2,2,2)  IS  4
```

Here is the game CODE-BREAKER to show single-dimensional arrays in use. The game is simple to play. The computer "thinks of" a four-digit number, and you have ten guesses to work it out. A correct digit in the wrong position within the code gives you a "white," while a correct digit in the correct position gives you a "black."

```
   10 REM CODE-BREAKER
   20 DIM C(4)
   30 DIM G(4)
   40 PRINT "I AM THINKING OF A 4
-DIGIT"
   50 PRINT "NUMBER, WHICH YOU HA
VE 10 GOES"
   60 PRINT "TO DISCOVER.   ALL 4
DIGITS ARE"
   70 PRINT "DIFFERENT. PRESS ANY
KEY"
   80 PRINT TAB 12;"TO BEGIN"
   90 PAUSE 4E4
  100 CLS
  110 LET C(1)=INT (RND*9)+1
  120 FOR Z=2 TO 4
  130 LET C(Z)=INT (RND*9)+1
  140 FOR J=1 TO Z-1
  150 IF C(J)=C(Z) THEN GOTO 130
  160 NEXT J
  170 NEXT Z
  180 FOR G=1 TO 10
  190 SCROLL
  200 PRINT TAB 8;"ENTER GUESS ";
G
  210 INPUT A
  220 LET A1=A
  230 FOR Z=1 TO 4
  240 LET G(Z)=A-10*INT (A/10)
  250 LET A=INT (A/10)
  260 NEXT Z
  270 LET B=0
  280 LET W=0
  290 FOR Z=1 TO 4
  300 IF C(Z)<>G(Z) THEN GOTO 330
  310 LET B=B+1
  320 LET G(Z)=0
  330 NEXT Z
  340 FOR Z=1 TO 4
  350 IF G(Z)=0 THEN GOTO 400
  360 FOR J=1 TO 4
  370 IF C(Z)<>G(J) THEN GOTO 390
  380 LET W=W+1
  390 NEXT J
  400 NEXT Z
  410 SCROLL
```

```
 420 PRINT A1;" SCORED ";CHR$ (B
+156);" BLACK";
 430 IF B<>1 THEN PRINT "S";
 440 PRINT ", ";W;" WHITE";
 450 IF W<>1 THEN PRINT "S"
 460 SCROLL
 470 IF B=4 THEN PRINT "YOU GUES
SED IT IN ";G;" GUESSES"
 480 IF B<>4 THEN NEXT G
 490 SCROLL
 500 PRINT TAB 5;"THE CODE WAS "
;C(4);C(3);C(2);C(1)
```

String arrays

You can also use string arrays, which are very similar to
numeric arrays. Enter and run the following program to see
the string array in practice, typing in four words (each followed by ENTER) when prompted.

```
10 REM STRING ARRAYS
20 DIM A$(4,10)
30 FOR B=1 TO 4
40 INPUT A$(B)
50 NEXT B
60 FOR B=1 TO 4
70 PRINT "A$(";B;") IS ";A$(B)
80 NEXT B
```

```
A$(1)  IS WATER
A$(2)  IS REASON
A$(3)  IS WASTE
A$(4)  IS ANGLOPHILE
```

Although the second number in the DIM statement (in this
case 10) has to be as long as the longest string you intend to
enter, you only need to specify the first element (as in line 70)
to get the full string to print out.

Note that the main difference between a string array and a
numeric array is the dollar sign immediately following the
letter. This tells the computer that the name refers to a string.

Here's a string sort program to show string arrays in use.
As set up, and as demonstrated in the sample run, the program caters for five words. To adapt it for more, change the
5 in lines 20, 30, and 40 to the number of words you need to
sort.

```
10 REM **STRING SORT**
20 DIM W$(5,10)
30 LET B=0
40 LET G=5
50 FOR A=1 TO 5
60 INPUT W$(A)
70 PRINT W$(A)
80 NEXT A
85 PRINT
90 LET Z=1
100 LET B=Z+1
110 IF B>G THEN GOTO 190
120 IF W$(B)>W$(Z) THEN GOTO 150
130 LET Z=Z+1
140 GOTO 100
150 LET Q$=W$(Z)
160 LET W$(Z)=W$(B)
170 LET W$(B)=Q$
180 GOTO 130
190 PRINT W$(G)
200 LET G=G-1
210 IF G>0 THEN GOTO 90
```

```
LATCH
BREATH
BREAD
DRAIN
DRAGON

BREAD
BREATH
DRAGON
DRAIN
LATCH
```

String handling

Our discussion of string arrays leads us neatly into strings
and string handling. As you've probably realized by now, a
string is a collection of alphanumeric characters within quotation
marks (including symbols and spaces, if desired). It is assigned to a variable whose name is a letter, followed by a
dollar sign. Strings are assigned in much the same way as are
numeric variables, by a statement of the form LET A$ =
''HI''.

We must look at the T/S 1000 *character set* before continuing
our discussion of string handling. The computer assigns a

unique number between 0 and 255 to everything the computer must print, from numbers, letters, and keywords, to symbols and operators. For example, the character of the letter A is 38. This means that if you told the computer to PRINT CHR$ 38 (and you'd do this by getting CHR$ from the U key, in the function mode), it would print the letter A.

You can see the full character set from 0 (the number for the space character) to 255 (which is the word COPY) by running the next program. Because the numbers from 67 to 126 are not used, or just print out as question marks, the program jumps over them.

```
10 REM CHARACTER SET
20 FOR A=0 TO 255
30 SCROLL
40 SCROLL
50 PRINT A;" ";CHR$ (A)
60 IF A=66 THEN LET A=127
70 NEXT A
```

There are a number of very useful string functions, which can be used for manipulation of strings and for extracting parts of the strings. The functions are:

**CODE X$** This gives the character code of the first character in X$, so if X$ equaled MICRO, CODE X$ would give 50.

CHR$ 66 We can check to see if, in fact, 50 is the code of the first letter of X$ (i.e., if it is the code of M) by asking the computer to PRINT CHR$ 66. This gives an M. In effect, CHR$ is the opposite of CODE, and turns a code back into a character.

X$ (TO 3) This gives a string containing the n leftmost characters of X$, so X$ (TO 3) will give "MIC".

**LEN X$** This function gives the length of a string; therefore, using our string, X$, of "MICRO", we get LEN X$ of 0.5.

X$ (n to m) This string function produces a string from X$ which lies between characters n and m, starting from character n. X$ (2 TO 4) gives "ICR".

X$ (n TO) This function gives the rightmost characters from n of the string, so X$ (2 TO), if X$ was MICRO, would give "ICRO".

STR8 A This turns a variable A into a string, so if the variable was 234, the string version would be "234". This may not seem to be much use but allows certain manipulation of numbers when they are strings which would be extremely difficult in their numeric form. We will look at STR8 in more detail shortly.

VAL X8 This is the "opposite" of STR8 A and takes the numeric value of the string and turns it into a number. Thus VAL X8, where X8 equals "22+34", would return 56.

Here is a printout from the computer showing the string functions in operation.

```
 10  PRINT "LET X$=""MICRO"""
 20  LET X$="MICRO"
 30  PRINT "CODE X$=";CODE X$
 40  PRINT "CHR$ 50=";CHR$ 50
 50  PRINT "X$(3 TO)=";X$(3 TO )
 60  PRINT "X$( TO 3)=";X$( TO 3
)
 70  PRINT "LEN X$=";LEN X$
 80  PRINT "X$(2 TO 4)=";X$(2 TO
 4)
 90  PRINT "LET X$=""23+35"""
100  LET X$="23+35"
110  PRINT "VAL X$=";VAL X$
120  PRINT "LET X=34"
130  LET X=34
140  PRINT "LET X$=STR$ X"
150  LET X$=STR$ X
160  PRINT "X$=";X$
```

```
LET X$="MICRO"
CODE X$=50
CHR$ 50=M
X$(3 TO)=CRO
X$( TO 3)=MIC
LEN X$=5
X$(2 TO 4)=ICR
LET X$="23+35"
VAL X$=58
LET X=34
LET X$=STR$ X
X$=34
```

PRINTing string arrays

Suppose you wanted a character array to hold the names of the months. There are 12 months in one year, and the name of the longest month is SEPTEMBER, which consists of nine letters. On your computer you would say

```
10 DIM A$(12,9)
```

to give you an array of 12 words each up to nine letters long. You would probably end up doing this:

```
20 FOR N=1 TO 12
30 INPUT A$(N)
40 NEXT N
```

and the variables could be saved on tape along with the program once you've entered all the data into the array. When you came to use the array, you would find that names which were less than nine letters long had been stretched out with spaces at the end to make them nine letters long to fit the array. So if you had the line

```
500 PRINT A$(5);" IS THE MONTH OF
YOUR BIRTHDAY"
```

you would end up with MAY   IS THE MONTH OF YOUR BIRTHDAY. All those extra spaces are ugly. It might not bother you with a word like DECEMBER, where you would get only one extra space, but with the word MAY you get six extra unwanted spaces, so we need to ensure that any trailing spaces (spaces after the word) are not PRINTed. Here is a routine to do this.

You will need to specify which part of the array is used—which word if you like—and this is represented by an X in the listing. Add these lines to the ones above:

```
490 INPUT X
500 GOSUB 6000
510 PRINT A$(X, TO A);" IS THE
MONTH OF YOUR BIRTHDAY"
520 STOP
8000 FOR A=LEN A$(X) TO 1 STEP -
1
8010 IF A$(X,A)<>" " THEN RETURN
8020 NEXT A
8030 RETURN
```

RUN the program and enter the names of the months one by one in order. As an experiment, try leaving one month as all spaces (just press ENTER for one name). You might expect an error to arise if A$(X) is composed entirely of spaces, but this is all catered for. If this does happen, then A will be 0 and A$(X, TO A) will be A$(X,1 TO 0). You might expect that this will give a subscript error, but the computer, as we've seen, has a special interpretation for this kind of expression (where the first figure in a string slice is larger than the second). You will end up with the empty string, so it will seem as though you don't have a birthday!

One small note. Look at line 510. It appears as though there's a number missing before TO. This is the same as A$(X,1 TO A) because if you leave out the number before TO, the computer will assume you meant 1. Don't forget to include the comma before TO.

Having RUN the program once, you should have all the names of the months in memory. When you want to use the program, use GOTO 490 to save having to retype the names of the months every time.

Using STR$

STR$ is a very useful and often neglected function. As we mentioned a few pages ago, it converts a number into its string equivalent, as it would appear when PRINTed on the screen. Try this program:

```
10 PRINT 2
20 PRINT STR$ 2
30 PRINT 1/3
40 PRINT STR$ (1/3)
50 PRINT 9E15
60 PRINT STR$ 9E15
```

You should get these results:

```
2
2
0.33333333
0.33333333
9E+15
9E+15
```

We can learn a lot from these examples. First, the string generated by STR$ is the same as you would get if you PRINTed the number on the screen. Second, numbers of less than 1 are assigned to a string with a 0 before the decimal point, providing the first digit after the decimal point is anything but 0 (i.e., the number is equal to or greater than 0.1 and less than 1), and there may be up to eight digits after the decimal point, although there may be less if all are not required. So there may be up to ten characters in the entire string. However, if the number to which STR$ is applied has more than eight digits after the decimal point, it is rounded off to eight decimal places, e.g., STR$ .333333339 becomes 0.33333334. STR$ is also capable of generating scientific notation (which you'll recall, we discussed earlier) such as 9E + 15. Note that although the computer accepts 9E15, STR$ assigns it as 9E + 15, that is, the exponent part is always signed. Very small numbers, e.g., Ø.ØØØØØ9 are assigned thus: STR$ 0.0000009 is 9E-7. When using STR$, it is often wise to limit the values of the number so that STR$ does not begin to use scientific notation, which will cause problems.

You are by now almost certainly thinking, fine, but what can you do with it? The main use is to convert numbers to strings so that we can apply the computer's string handling facilities for formatting or rounding off to a given number of decimal places or other purposes where you need to be able to assess a number digit by digit. Here are some examples of the application of STR$.

Suppose you had a list of numbers to print and you wanted to line up decimal points. Try this program:

```
10 LET A=RND*100
20 PRINT A
30 LET A=A*10
40 GOTO 20
```

You should get something like this:

```
8.581543
85.81543
858.1543
8581.543
```

107-2

It would be much more legible and readable if we could

line up the decimal points, and this is often very useful. Try this routine:

```
10 LET A=RND*100
20 PRINT TAB 15-LEN STR$ INT A
;A
30 LET A=A*10
40 GOTO 20
```

This spaces everything out so that the decimal points appear beneath each other. It's very useful for a chart or list of numbers where you may wish to quickly compare several numbers. Can you see how the program works? Suppose the value of A was 69.433594. What the program does is take the integer part of A (INT A, which is 69), converts this to a string (STR$ INT A), then measures the length of this string (LEN STR$ INT A) which in this case is 2. It then uses the number to work out how far back across the screen to start PRINTing the value of A. Note how this is done:

```
TAB 15-LEN STR$ INT A
```

This means that 15 is how far across the screen the decimal point is placed, and then it counts back by the number of digits in STR$ INT A.

Another application of STR$ is if you needed to PRINT to a given number of decimal places. You will remember that the above example printed numbers with all the digits known. We can use STR$ to regulate how many numbers are PRINTed after the decimal point. Consider this routine:

```
10 LET A=RND*100
20 LET A$=STR$ A
22 IF A$(1)="." THEN LET A$="0
"+A$
25 LET B=LEN STR$ INT VAL A$
27 PRINT TAB 15-B;(A$+("." AND
B=LEN A$)+"000")( TO B+4)
30 LET A=A*10
40 GOTO 20
```

This will PRINT to three decimal places, adding both leading zeros (0 at beginning) and trailing zeros (0 at end) if required. To get it to PRINT to Z decimal places, make the following changes to line 27: add as many spaces to A$ as the number of decimal places you require (i.e., Z zeros), and you should make the slicer statement (TO B + 1 + Z).

Here is a line by line explanation:

Line 10 sets the value of A to start off with.

Line 20 converts A to a string.

Line 22 adds a 0 before the first digit if it is a decimal point. Unfortunately, the STR$ function is not uniform in its action in that it sometimes supplies a leading 0 for numbers less than 1 and sometimes doesn't, depending on whether the first digit after the decimal point is 0. Therefore, it is a simple matter to check if a 0 is required or not—if the first character is a decimal point, add a 0.

Line 25 sets B equal to the integer part of the number represented by A$.

Line 27 spaces the PRINT position, then sets about PRINTing A$ to three decimal places. First of all, A$ is PRINTed complete, then a decimal point is added if A$ already represents a whole number and enough zeros to make up three decimal places. You may be wondering why you should add 4 to B—surely we're PRINTing to three decimal places? Remember the decimal point—that's an extra character! For the purpose of the slicing statement, the part before is treated as one long string, provided it is all in parentheses. All we've done is add characters to pad out A$ to at least three decimal places, then PRINT up to three digits after the decimal point. This routine does not round off the third decimal place. There is a routine in the SNIPPETS section to do that.

Another function of strings is to save memory. It is often possible to save memory by using strings to hold numbers, instead of numeric variables, and decode them later using VAL. You can store a number in a string variable using STR$:

```
LET A$=STR$ (1024)
```

and decode it later as required using VAL:

```
PRINT VAL A$
```

You will often find that you use up more memory in converting numbers in this fashion than you would in using proper numeric variables, but sometimes this method can work wonders!

Try applying VAL to an expression like "ATN 1 × 4". It

works, and this is often quite a useful facility. You can have the name of a numeric variable in quotes, and, provided it has previously been defined or assigned, it will be successfully evaluated.

It may also be useful if you wish to generate random numbers several times in a program. At the start of the program have a statement line LET A$ = "RND*6", and every time you wanted a random number you would type LET R = VAL A$.

INKEYS

You do not need to press ENTER after pressing a key when INKEY$ is used, as our next program makes clear.

Try the following. Enter a number from 1 to 9, by pressing the key of that number, and you'll see it print out YOU PRESSED 6, YOU PRESSED 1, and so on. Touch the zero key to end, and it will print out YOU PRESSED Ø and then stop.

```
10 REM ** INKEY$ DEMO **
20 IF INKEY$<>"" THEN GOTO 20
30 IF INKEY$="" THEN GOTO 30
35 LET A$=INKEY$
40 PRINT "YOU PRESSED ";A$
50 IF A$="0" THEN STOP
60 GOTO 20

YOU PRESSED 1
YOU PRESSED 6
YOU PRESSED 3
YOU PRESSED 5
YOU PRESSED 2
YOU PRESSED 4
YOU PRESSED 3
YOU PRESSED 8
YOU PRESSED 4
YOU PRESSED 0
```

The next program—PREDICTION—also uses INKEYS. In this game, you have to try and anticipate the number (from 1 to 9) that the computer will select. The computer's number is shown on the screen near the middle, and the lowest number is the score. The lower the score at the end (when you manage to successfully predict the computer's number), the better. The screen will stay blank until you press a key. The words "THE SCORE IS" will flash off and on at the end. You can see how line 13Ø does this. Note also lines 5Ø and 6Ø which wait (5Ø) till no key is being pressed, and, once the keyboard is clear, waits (6Ø) for a key to be pressed.

```
    YOUR NUMBER IS 9


      MY NUMBER IS 9

      THE SCORE IS 23
```

```
 10 REM #*PREDICTION"
 20 LET E=9
 40 LET Q=0
 50 IF INKEY$<>"" THEN GOTO 50
 60 IF INKEY$="" THEN GOTO 60
 70 LET A$=INKEY$
 80 PRINT AT 8,5;"YOUR NUMBER I
S ";A$
 90 LET Q=Q+1
110 LET W$=STR$ (INT (RND*9)+1)
120 PRINT AT 12,E;"MY NUMBER IS
";W$
130 PRINT AT 14,E;"THE SCORE IS
";Q;AT 14,E;"THE SCORE IS "
140 IF W$=A$ THEN GOTO 130
150 GOTO 50
```

The next program—MAZE MAKER—also shows INKEY$ in action. Using the A, Z, K, and M keys, you have to move the $ sign from the bottom left-hand corner to the top right-hand one, without crossing any of the little white squares. Note that no path through is guaranteed, and there is no mechanism for checking that you don't cheat. At the end, the number of "moves" you took is printed on the board.

```
10 REM **MAZE MAKER**
20 REM USE THE A Z M K KEYS
30 REM TO MOVE THE $ SIGN
40 REM FROM THE BOTTOM
50 REM LEFT-HAND CORNER TO THE
60 REM TOP RIGHT. NO PATH THRU
```

```
 70 REM IS GUARANTEED
 80 LET S=0
 90 FOR Y=1 TO 700
100 LET T=INT (RND*3)
110 PRINT ("█" AND T=0)+(" " AN
D T>0);
120 NEXT Y
130 PRINT AT 0,0;"   ";AT 1,0;"
"
140 LET X=30
145 LET Y=19
150 LET M=X
160 LET N=Y
170 PRINT AT Y,X;"$"
180 LET S=S+1
190 LET A$=INKEY$
200 IF A$="" THEN GOTO 190
210 IF A$="A" AND Y>0 THEN LET
Y=Y-1
220 IF A$="Z" AND Y<20 THEN LET
Y=Y+1
230 IF A$="K" AND X<31 THEN LET
X=X+1
240 IF A$="M" AND X>0 THEN LET
X=X-1
250 IF X=0 AND Y=0 THEN GOTO 28
0
260 PRINT AT N,M;" "
270 GOTO 150
280 SCROLL
290 PRINT "YOU MADE IT"
300 SCROLL
310 PRINT "IT TOOK YOU ";S;" MO
VES"
320 GOTO 280
```

Note in line 110 how use is made of the computer's logic methods of evaluation. This line ensures that if T (generated in the previous line) is 0, a black square is printed, and a blank space is generated if T is greater than 0. This is a memory-efficient way of emulating the IF/THEN/ELSE command available on some other computers. This technique, and similar ones, are discussed in greater detail elsewhere in the book.

Because it can take quite a long time for the maze to be drawn, you may prefer to set up the maze in the FAST mode, and then display it for you to solve in SLOW. You can do this by adding 15 FAST and 125 SLOW.

The next program—ROAD RUNNER—shows INKEY$ in

action again. In this program you are attempting to drive a long line of letter V's down a twisting, turning track of black blobs. Your controls are Z and M which move you left and right respectively.

Lines 55 and 60 move the track randomly, making sure that it does not stray off the edge of the screen. Line 70 prints the V, which is scrolled up (as is the track) by line 80. Line 100 checks the status of the position that V will next occupy, and if it finds a 128 there (character 128 is the blob) sends action to line 140.

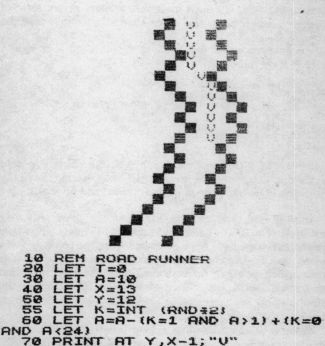

```
10 REM ROAD RUNNER
20 LET T=0
30 LET A=10
40 LET X=13
50 LET Y=12
55 LET K=INT (RND*2)
60 LET A=A-(K=1 AND A>1)+(K=0
AND A<24)
70 PRINT AT Y,X-1;"V"
80 SCROLL
90 PRINT TAB A;"█";TAB A+5;"█"
95 PRINT AT Y+1,X-1;
100 IF PEEK (PEEK 16398+PEEK 16
399*256)=128 THEN GOTO 140
```

```
 110 LET X=X-(INKEY$="Z" AND X>2
)+(INKEY$="M" AND X<32)
 120 LET T=T+1
 130 GOTO 55
 140 PRINT AT Y,X-1;"V"
 150 PRINT AT 6,8;"YOU HAVE CRAS
HED"
 160 PRINT AT 8,10;"YOU SCORED "
;T
 170 PRINT AT 6,8;"YOU HAVE CRAS
HED"
 180 GOTO 150
```

If you want a time limit on user responses, you can use the following method. Suppose the user has only a short time, say two seconds, in which to decide whether or not to have another game. If he or she is too slow in deciding, then the program stops.

For the purpose of this routine, suppose the user has to press R for a rerun:

```
10 FOR F=1 TO 55
20 LET A$=INKEY$
30 IF A$="R" THEN GOTO 60
40 NEXT F
50 STOP
60 PRINT "RE-RUN"
70 RUN
```

In view of a previous paragraph, you may have expected to have a loop of 120 in line 10, but having anything inside the FOR/NEXT loop slows it down, and 55 is adequate in this case.

Alternatively, you can make use of the *frame counter*, part of the T/S 1000's inner workings which counts how many television frames have been generated since the computer was turned on. To use the frame counter, you need to reset it to 0, which you can do with the following (and note that we discuss PEEK and POKE in detail a little later in the book):

```
POKE 16437,255
POKE 16436,255
```

To see its value (to know how much time has elapsed) at any time later on during the program, use:

```
     LET T=(65536-PEEK 16436-256
*PEEK 16437)/50
```

Here's an example. Lines 10 and 20 set the timer to 0, and lines 30 and 40 wait for you to press any key (except SHIFT or BREAK). When you do touch a key, line 50 prints out the time (in seconds) which has elapsed since you started the program running. It is not totally accurate, as the computer takes a fraction of a second to work out the expression, and a little longer to print out the result, but it is close enough for most purposes. (Keep in mind that the PAUSE command uses the frame counter, so you can't use PAUSE in a program where you're using this timer.)

```
10 POKE 16437,255
20 POKE 16436,255
30 IF INKEY$<>"" THEN GOTO 30
40 IF INKEY$="" THEN GOTO 40
50 LET T=(65536-PEEK 16436-256
*PEEK 16437)/50
60 PRINT AT 4,4;T
70 GOTO 30
```

CHAPTER 12
Displays

Clearing a part of the display

There is a useful subroutine that enables you to clear any number of lines from the bottom of the screen. It enables the instructions to be kept on the top few lines of the display during the game, or the score or any other special instructions may be kept on screen while everything else is cleared. The subroutine should be called by GOSUB 8000.

```
10 FOR I=1 TO 416
20 PRINT "■";
30 NEXT I

8000 PRINT AT 21,0;"HOW MANY LIN
ES TO BE CLEARED?"
8010 INPUT C
8020 IF C<0 OR C>21 THEN GOTO 80
10
8030 FOR F=21 TO 21-C STEP -1
8040 PRINT AT F,0;"                "
8050 NEXT F
8060 PRINT AT F+1,0;
8070 RETURN
```

Line 8000 asks how many lines you want to clear, starting from line 21 at the bottom of the screen and working upward. It looks quite impressive! The INPUT statement in line 8010 is not idiot-proofed; you may want to experiment with this yourself. The statement in line 8060 moves the PRINT position to the start of the part of the screen you've just cleared.

Screen SCROLLing in BASIC

The only method that can be realistically used to SCROLL the screen is to store an image of the screen in a string array and PRINT this. Here are four example programs that enable the entire screen to be SCROLLed up, down, left, or right.

Note that these programs will not fit into the standard T/S 1000. You can use them only if you have additional memory fitted. You'll see how effective these programs can be when you run them. Enter at least three lines of text (as a result of the input prompt from line 20) to see the routines at their best.

These routines are noticeably slower than the command SCROLL, especially the left and right SCROLLs because those are PRINTed one line at a time.

Upward SCROLL:

```
10 DIM A$(704)
20 INPUT A$
30 PRINT AT 0,0;A$
40 LET A$=A$(33 TO )+"
              "
50 GOTO 30
```

Downward SCROLL:

```
10 DIM A$(704)
20 INPUT A$
30 PRINT AT 0,0;A$
40 LET A$="
              "+A$( TO 672)
50 GOTO 30
```

Leftward SCROLL:

```
10 DIM A$(704)
20 INPUT A$
30 PRINT AT 0,0;A$
40 FOR F=1 TO 673 STEP 32
50 LET A$(F TO F+31)=A$(F+1 TO
F+31)+" "
60 NEXT F
70 GOTO 30
```

Rightward SCROLL:

```
10 DIM A$(704)
20 INPUT A$
30 PRINT AT 0,0;A$
40 FOR F=1 TO 673 STEP 32
50 LET A$(F TO F+31)=" "+A$(F
TO F+30)
60 NEXT F
70 GOTO 30
```

Saving lines at screen edges

The easiest way to accomplish this is to use the string slicing facility to SCROLL certain parts of the string only. Here is an example with the upward SCROLL. L is the number of lines NOT to be SCROLLed. It is better to put at least three lines of text when asked.

```
10 DIM A$(704)
20 INPUT A$
25 INPUT L
30 PRINT AT 0,0;A$
40 LET A$(L*32+1 TO )=A$((L+1)
*32+1 TO )
50 GOTO 30
```

A similar program can be used with the downward SCROLL. L is the number of lines not to be SCROLLed at the bottom of the screen.

```
10 DIM A$(704)
20 INPUT A$
25 INPUT L
30 PRINT AT 0,0;A$
40 LET A$( TO 704-L*32)="
            "+A$(
TO 704-(L+1)*32)
50 GOTO 30
```

The same technique can be applied to the sideways SCROLLs, but since these are slow enough already, it hardly seems worthwhile. You can extend this idea to permit lines in any part of the screen to be kept stationary while those above and/or below are SCROLLed, simply by modifying the string slicing; however, if you require complex arithmetic to work this out, then you may slow the routine down excessively.

Another technique you can apply to these routines is *wraparound*, whereby anything disappearing off any edge promptly reappears on the opposite edge. Here's how to do this with an upward SCROLL:

```
10 DIM A$(704)
20 INPUT A$
30 PRINT AT 0,0;A$
40 LET A$=A$(33 TO )+A$( TO 32
)
50 GOTO 30
```

a downward SCROLL with wraparound:

```
10 DIM A$(704)
20 INPUT A$
30 PRINT AT 0,0;A$
40 LET A$=A$(673 TO )+A$( TO 6
72)
50 GOTO 30
```

and a leftward SCROLL with wraparound:

```
10 DIM A$(704)
20 INPUT A$
30 PRINT AT 0,0;A$
40 FOR F=1 TO 673 STEP 32
50 LET A$(F TO F+31)=A$(F+1 TO
F+31)+A$(F)
60 NEXT F
70 GOTO 30
```

For a rightward SCROLL with wraparound, change line 50 to

```
50 LET A$(F TO F+31)=A$(F+31)+
A$(F TO F+30)
```

Keep in mind that the routines are not SCROLLing PRINT statements, but moving elements of the array A$. Therefore, you cannot just PRINT something to the screen and expect it to be SCROLLed. Instead, you must assign elements of the array to the letters you wish to SCROLL. Here's an example, which allows you to input additional string information after the first array has been entered. It uses the downward SCROLL with wraparound routine. When you run it, you are able to enter a string as before. Then, you interrupt the downward SCROLLing at any point by touching any key (except BREAK or SHIFT). You then enter a new string, and press ENTER, and your new material starts SCROLLing down from the top, while the original material continues its downward SCROLL. You can do this over and over again, noting that you'll *overwrite* information which is at the very top of the screen when you decide to input new material. Run this, and it should be clear:

```
 10 DIM A$(704)
 20 INPUT A$
 30 PRINT AT 0,0;A$
 40 LET A$=A$(673 TO )+A$( TO 6
72)
 50 IF INKEY$<>"" THEN GOTO 80
 60 GOTO 30
 80 INPUT B$
 90 LET A$=B$+A$(LEN B$+1 TO 70
4)
100 GOTO 30
```

CHAPTER 13
Moving graphics

The theory behind moving graphics is that first we draw a character in one position for a short time, then erase it and draw it in another position. Variables are used to remember the position of the character. Let us look at an example program which we can draw up from this theory:

```
10 LET X=0
20 PRINT AT 5,X; "█"
30 PRINT AT 5,X; " "
40 LET X=X+1
50 GOTO 20
```

This is not a very good program—the black blob seems to flash on and off as it moves across the screen and the program stops with report B/20 when the blob reaches the right-hand side of the screen. If you look up what the error report means in the appendix of this book, it says that the integer is out of range. What has happened is that X was the variable that told the computer how far across the screen it should PRINT the black blob, and if the number is greater than 31, then your computer cannot PRINT since the limits of the screen are from 0 to 31, and any attempts to use a number greater than 31 would place the blob off the screen to the right. Now the T/S 1000, being a rather clever little machine, decides that this is an error, so it stops the program and tells you what went wrong so that you can correct it. Let us do this. The easiest way is to arrange that if the value of X goes outside the permitted range, then the program automatically changes it to a suitable value. One way in which this can be done is to add a line like

```
45 IF X>31 THEN LET X=0
```

but since we already have a line saying LET X=0 in line 10,

we could do the same thing by sending the program back to line 1Ø:

```
45 IF X>31 THEN GOTO 10
```

The technique of sending a program back to the beginning in order to reset some variables to their starting values is used rather a lot in programs. In this example both methods achieve the same results, but you may come across certain programs where only one is suitable, or one method is better than the other.

The next step is to improve the flashing display. One way to do this is to make sure the blob is displayed for longer than it is erased. Try this:

```
10 LET X=0
20 PRINT AT 5,X; "█"
30 FOR F=1 TO 5
40 NEXT F
50 PRINT AT 5,X; " "
60 LET X=X+1
70 IF X>31 THEN LET X=0
80 GOTO 20
```

It seems to work rather well, but in most programs there are other computations to be carried out which will slow down the program, and the time-wasting loop of lines 3Ø and 4Ø will slow things down unnecessarily. Therefore, this is not a very good approach. Let us try to reduce the flashing by reducing the time between the space being PRINTed and the blob being PRINTed. Try this program:

```
10 LET X=0
20 LET P=X
30 LET X=X+1
40 IF X>31 THEN LET X=0
50 PRINT AT 5,P; " "; AT 5,X; "█"
60 GOTO 20
```

Here, X is the variable that remembers the current position of the blob. P remembers the previous position so that it may be erased by drawing a space over it. Line 1Ø makes X start off with a value of 0. Line 2Ø determines the value of P by making it equal to X *before* X is increased in value in line 3Ø. This can be any amount of increase—try changing the number after the + sign to see the effect. It appears to move faster, and that can be advantageous or disadvantageous. Stay with 1 after the + sign for now.

Line 40 ensures that when the blob has reached the right-hand side of the screen, it is sent back to the left-hand side of the screen by resetting X to 0. This provides a constant supply of blobs for us! Line 50 does all the PRINTing—note how two AT functions can be placed on the same line joined by a semicolon. We can also do the same with TAB incidentally. Try writing these as two separate lines like this to see if it makes any difference to the program:

```
50 PRINT AT 5,P; " "
55 PRINT AT 5,X; "■"
```

We can shorten the program by one line by changing line 30 to

```
30 LET X=X+1 AND X<31
```

The way in which this line works is rather complex, and is more fully explained in the sections on conditional statements. Simplified, it means ''if X is less than 31, then add 1 to the value of X, but if X is not less than 31, then make X 0.'' Now delete line 40 (the one we've made redundant), and renumber nicely in steps of 10; we should end up with this:

```
10 LET X=0
20 LET P=X
30 LET X=X+1 AND X<31
40 PRINT AT 5,P; " ";AT 5,X; "■"
50 GOTO 20
```

You may have noticed that the space is PRINTed one column behind the blob all the time, and therefore it may be possible to simply use PRINT AT 5,X; ''(space)■'' and dispense with the variable P altogether. This does make the display smoother, but it causes problems when it gets to the end of the line and you need an extra line to clear this position. To see what I mean, try this program:

```
10 LET X=0
20 LET X=X+1 AND X<30
30 PRINT AT 5,X; " ■"
40 GOTO 20
```

Note that every time a new blob shoots across the screen, the old one stays on the right of the screen. Let us add a facility to erase these blobs:

```
10 LET X=0
20 LET X=X+1 AND X<30
30 PRINT AT 5,X;" ■"
35 IF X=0 THEN PRINT AT 5,31;"
"
40 GOTO 20
```

Again we can use AND to shorten the program a little:

```
10 LET X=0
20 LET X=X+1 AND X<30
30 PRINT AT 5,X;" ■";AT 5,31;"
" AND X=0
40 GOTO 20
```

Line 35 in the first program and the second part of line 30 in the second program ensure that a space is only PRINTed if the blob has reached the end of its travel. Here is another way of doing this using the control variable of a FOR/NEXT loop instead of the conventional variable X. This method uses a little less memory and is slightly faster to run.

```
10 FOR X=0 TO 30
20 PRINT AT 5,X;" ■";AT 5,31;"
" AND X=0
30 NEXT X
40 GOTO 10
```

Another way to use this method is to have PRINT AT 5,31; "(space)" outside the FOR/NEXT loop. This has the advantage that the computer does not have to examine the conditional expression as often; therefore, the program runs slightly faster:

```
10 FOR X=0 TO 30
20 PRINT AT 5,X;" ■"
30 NEXT X
40 PRINT AT 5,31;" "
50 GOTO 10
```

We've ended up with a routine that is quite fast-running and economical in memory usage. We've also seen some of the problems of developing this kind of program. The examples we've seen so far deal with constant movement across the screen. We will also want to move characters about the screen, possibly with control of this movement from the keyboard so that the operator may control the movement. To do this, we first need to return to INKEY$, a very useful aid for moving graphics. If you've read the earlier section, you'll recall that INKEY$ is the character which corresponds to the key being pressed on the keyboard. If you press K, then INKEY$ is "K" or INKEY$ = "K". If you aren't pressing anything on the keyboard, INKEY$ becomes the empty string, or " ". (INKEY$ cannot be "(space)" because pressing SPACE acts as BREAK when a program is running and stops a BASIC program.) We will look now at some other ways in which we can use INKEY$, because it is a powerful and extremely useful function for moving graphics. Most arcade games require you to press buttons, flick switches or manipulate joysticks. Your computer does not have these (unless you buy or build an add-on board), so all control has to be through the keyboard.

To control movement on the screen, certain keys have advantages over others, either because of their layout or because of what's written on them. For instance, take the M and the N keys on the bottom row of the keyboard. They have the < and > symbols marked on them in red. These can be considered as arrows pointing left or right, so they could be used to control left/right movement on screen, e.g., in an invaders type of game. Their advantage is that they are easy to find and are next to each other, making them convenient to use. One disadvantage is that they are near the BREAK key, and you may accidentally stop the program in a frenzied hurry to avoid being bombed by the green menace.

If you want to control left/right/up/down movement (e.g., to move the cursor in the word-processor program near the back of this book), then the 5, 6, 7, and 8 keys are a better choice since they have arrows pointing in the four directions printed on the keys and are next to each other for convenience of use but are not dangerously near BREAK.

The most common way of using INKEY$ in a moving graphics program (be it games or serious applications) is to put it in a conditional statement to control the value of a variable. For example,

```
IF INKEY$="8" THEN LET X=X+1
```

Here, 1 is added to the value of X if the 8 key is being pressed, but X stays the same if no key is being pressed or a key other than 8 is being pressed. The variable can

be used to control, for example, where to PRINT on the
screen:

```
100 IF INKEY$="5" THEN LET X=X-
1
110 IF INKEY$="8" THEN LET X=X-
1
120 IF INKEY$="7" THEN LET Y=Y-
1
130 IF INKEY$="6" THEN LET Y=Y+
1
140 PRINT AT Y,X;"*"
```

If we adopt the convention of X being the horizontal
position across the screen and Y being the vertical position on
the screen, then the larger the value of X, the further to
the right across the screen the character is PRINTed, and the
larger the value of Y, the further down the screen the character is PRINTed.

Knowing this we can write a short program to control the
movement of a character (e.g., an asterisk) on the screen
using the keys 5, 6, 7, and 8 (the keys with arrows printed on
them):

```
100 IF INKEY$="5" THEN LET X=X-
1
110 IF INKEY$="8" THEN LET X=X+
1
120 IF INKEY$="7" THEN LET Y=Y-
1
130 IF INKEY$="6" THEN LET Y=Y+
1
140 PRINT AT Y,X;" "
```

Before we can RUN this program we need to define X and
Y or we'll cause an error 2 when the computer tries to carry
out any of the lines. Add these lines to the program:

```
10 LET X=0
20 LET Y=0
```

We can now RUN the program. What we get is an asterisk
PRINTed at the top left corner of the screen, and the program
stops after line 140. To prevent this from happening, we can
add a line like

```
200 GOTO 100
```

This ensures that the computer continues doing the task

over and over again. RUN the program and try pressing the 5, 6, 7, and 8 keys one at a time. You will see that as the asterisk moves it leaves behind a trail of asterisks. Keep going to the edge of the screen and keep pressing the keys. Strange things begin to happen. If you go off the bottom of the screen or off the right-hand side of the screen, the program stops with error B in line 140. This is because the value of X has become greater than 31 or the value of Y has become greater than 21, and as a consequence the computer is being asked to PRINT outside the screen boundaries—this, of course, it cannot do.

However, if you try to move past the top of the screen or the left-hand edge of the screen, even stranger things begin to happen—the asterisk starts to travel in the opposite direction! It's not that we've broken the computer or anything like that; there is a simple explanation. When the value of X or Y is negative (as happens when you try to go off the top or the left-hand side of the screen), then PRINT ignores the − sign (it takes the ABS value if you like), and it apparently causes some keys to change functions! Not very useful to say the least, since you then have to take the asterisk back to the screen boundaries to restore normal operation. What we need is a method whereby if the asterisk gets to the edge of the screen it stops and will not attempt to go outside the screen line.

The easiest method is to prevent X and Y taking values which cause these problems. The values which are permissible are 0 to 31 for X and 0 to 21 for Y. Here's how to do this. Change lines 100, 110, 120, and 130 like this:

```
100 IF INKEY$="5" AND X>0 THEN
LET X=X-1
110 IF INKEY$="8" AND X<31 THEN
LET X=X+1
120 IF INKEY$="7" AND Y>0 THEN
LET Y=Y-1
130 IF INKEY$="6" AND Y<21 THEN
LET Y=Y+1
```

This makes the asterisk stay on the screen properly, but we still have a problem in that a trail of asterisks is set up as the asterisk moves. This is because we have no facility to erase the old position of the asterisk when it moves. The best way to do this is to use a second set of variables to remember the old position of the character, and if it's different than the new position, to PRINT a space in the old position.

To do this add these lines:

```
 50 LET A=X
 60 LET B=Y
135 IF A<>X OR B<>Y THEN PRINT
AT B,A;" "
200 GOTO 50
```

The program you have in the computer should now be:

```
 10 LET X=0
 20 LET Y=0
 50 LET A=X
 60 LET B=Y
100 IF INKEY$="5" AND X>0 THEN
LET X=X-1
110 IF INKEY$="8" AND X<31 THEN
LET X=X+1
120 IF INKEY$="7" AND Y>0 THEN
LET Y=Y-1
130 IF INKEY$="6" AND Y<21 THEN
LET Y=Y+1
135 IF A<>X OR B<>Y THEN PRINT
AT B,A;" "
140 PRINT AT Y,X;"*"
200 GOTO 50
```

We now have learned the basics of a moving graphics program. When we get around to designing a game around this routine, we may have to alter some details or change the order of statements but the principles involved will be similar. As we did earlier, we may also be able to shorten the routine somewhat, for example:

```
 10 LET X=0
 20 LET Y=0
 50 LET A=X
 60 LET B=Y
100 LET X=X-(INKEY$="5" AND X>0
)+(INKEY$="8" AND X<31)
110 LET Y=Y-(INKEY$="7" AND Y>0
)+(INKEY$="6" AND Y<21)
135 IF A<>X OR B<>Y THEN PRINT
AT B,A;" "
140 PRINT AT Y,X;"*"
200 GOTO 50
```

This version occupies nearly 50 bytes less than the previous version. You could also combine line 140 with line 135 into one conditional statement, since neither PRINT statement is required unless the asterisk has moved. This means we can delete line 140. Here is how to change line 135:

```
135 IF A<>X OR B<>Y THEN PRINT
AT B,A;" ";AT Y,X;"*"
```

Remember to delete line 140. The disadvantage is that while saving 5 more bytes of memory, when the program is first RUN, the asterisk does not actually appear on screen until it is moved! So it is better not to do this unless you are desperate for memory!

Let us now look at another facility which is useful in moving graphics programs—SCROLL. The action of SCROLL is to move everything in the display up one line; if there was anything printed on the top line of the display then it is lost. When SCROLL has been used, the PRINT position is moved to start of the bottom line, i.e., PRINT AT 21,0;, by the computer. You can move the PRINT position elsewhere if you choose by means of another PRINT AT statement.

Can you see how we could make use of SCROLL when writing programs with moving graphics? Take the example of a game where the spaceship is rushing through space, with asteroids or space debris rushing past. The only problem is to keep the spaceship still. To see how we do this, study the game program CRASHER that follows.

In general, moving-graphics programs using SCROLL tend to take this form: A character is placed at a certain position on the screen and other characters SCROLL up the screen towards it, the object being to control sideways movement of the first character so that it hits or avoids those being SCROLLed up toward it. This leads us to an important requirement—to be able to tell whether something has been hit, missed, or whatever. The method we actually use is as follows:

First, move the PRINT position to where we want to examine but don't actually PRINT anything there. Then look up the memory location to see what's already there. This may be done more simply than it sounds. The system variables 16398 and 16399 which store the address of the PRINT position in the display file (the area of memory which stores the picture) are very useful for this purpose. What we do is move the PRINT position somewhere without printing anything there (using PRINT AT Y,X; for example, without anything after the semicolon), then find the address of the PRINT position in the display file by using PEEK(PEEK 16398 + 256*PEEK 16399), i.e., PEEKing the address of the PRINT position which is given by the expression in parentheses and analyzing the number obtained. This can be seen better by analyzing the program CRASHER that we'll look at shortly. First, though, here are a few sample programs to illustrate other moving-graphics ideas we've discussed. For further explanation, see the section on PEEK and POKE.

UFO

The object of this game is to fire, by pressing any key except BREAK, when the UFO flies over your base, and be rewarded with a hit if you succeed. You only have 10 shots so try to score as many hits as possible before the game stops.

Here is the listing:

```
10 PRINT AT 15,14;"▄▆▄";AT 4,0
;"         HITS: 0            "
20 LET H=0
30 LET M=H
40 LET Y=RND*6+7
50 FOR X=0 TO 19
70 IF H+M=10 THEN STOP
80 PRINT AT Y,X;" ▇"
90 IF INKEY$<>"" AND X=14 THEN
GOTO 140
100 IF INKEY$<>"" THEN LET M=M+
1
110 NEXT X
120 PRINT AT Y,20;"  "
130 GOTO 40
140 LET H=H+1
150 FOR F=1 TO 30
160 PRINT AT Y,X;"HIT";AT Y,X;"
▇▇▇";AT Y,X;"   "
170 NEXT F
180 PRINT AT 4,12;H
190 GOTO 40
```

HITS: 02

Line 10 sets up the main parts of the display, the parts that do not move during the program. H is the variable that remembers the amount of hits you have scored and M the amount of misses (shots without hitting the UFO!), and both are initially set to 0. Line 40 sets the Y coordinate of the UFO to a value from 7 to 13 at random. PRINT takes the value of the nearest whole number if one of the coordinates is not an integer, so RND*6 + 7 can be from 7 to 13. This gives the position of the UFO up the screen. The main loop for controlling the flight of the UFO across the screen begins at line 50; 0 is the starting position, 19 the end position. Line 70 checks if you've had 10 shots, then stops the program if you have. Line 80 PRINTs the UFO, an inverse +. Note how it erases the old position by PRINTing a space one position behind the UFO (in its previous position). Line 90 checks if a key is being pressed, and if the UFO is directly above the base, it sends the action to the HIT routine at line 140. This adds 1 to the number of hits scored and provides an explosive-looking display at the point where the UFO was hit, then sends the program to line 40 again to supply another UFO. However, if a key was pressed and the UFO was not above the base, then 1 is added to the number of misses. If the UFO reaches the end of its travel, the program falls out of the FOR/NEXT loop and line 120 erases the final position of the

UFO; then line 13Ø sends the program back to line 4Ø to set up a new UFO.

Garbage gobbler

The object of this game is to clear up garbage which appears on the screen as little gray squares. You control the inverse + with the 5, 6, 7, and 8 keys, movement being in the direction of the arrows printed on the keys. You collect the garbage by landing on top of it. You can only move over a small section of the screen, because the program has been designed to RUN on a standard T/S 1000, so users with more memory can expand the program to cover a greater area of the screen if they desire. You are given a random time, and you are told how many items of garbage you collected when this time is up. The loop in lines 1Ø to 3Ø sets up the garbage in random positions.

```
   1 RAND
  10 FOR A=1 TO 20
  20 PRINT AT INT (RND*15),INT (
RND*17);CHR$ 8
  30 NEXT A
  40 LET A=0
  50 LET X=INT (RND*17)
  60 LET Y=INT (RND*15)
  70 FOR T=INT (RND*80)+30 TO 0
STEP -1
  80 LET X1=X
  90 LET Y1=Y
 100 LET X=X+(INKEY$="8" AND X<1
6)-(INKEY$="5" AND X>0)
 110 LET Y=Y+(INKEY$="6" AND Y<1
4)-(INKEY$="7" AND Y>0)
 120 PRINT AT Y,X;
 130 IF PEEK (PEEK 16398+256*PEE
K 16399)=8 THEN LET A=A+1
 140 PRINT AT Y1,X1;" " AND (X<>
X1 OR Y<>Y1);AT Y,X;"█"
 150 NEXT T
 160 PRINT AT 20,0;"YOU COLLECTE
D ";A
```

YOU COLLECTED 12

You can vary the amount of garbage PRINTed by changing the number after TO in line 1Ø A is the amount of garbage collected and is initially set to 0 in line 4Ø. Lines 5Ø and 6Ø set the initial position of the ▣. Line 7Ø sets the timing loop to a random value between 3Ø and 11Ø and counts backwards to Ø (STEP -1). In lines 8Ø and 9Ø a second set of variables X1 and Y1 remember the position of the ▣ so that if it moves we know where to erase. Lines 1ØØ and 11Ø detect which keys are pressed and change the values of X and Y accordingly; they also set the limits of travel. Line 12Ø moves the PRINT position to the new location of the ▣. Line 13Ø picks up the address of this position in memory from the system variables 16398 and 16399, then PEEKs this address to find out if there is garbage there and adds 1 to A if there is. Line 14Ø erases the old position of the ▣ if it's different from the new position and places it in its new position. If your time is up (the program has fallen out of the FOR/NEXT loop), then line 16Ø tells you how many items of garbage you collected.

Crasher

The name of this program has nothing to do with some computers' habits of blanking out! You are drifting in space, the object being to clear up as much debris as you can, particularly debris with a high code value. The debris is valued according to the code of the character of debris. The letters score highest, then numbers, and so on. Have a look at the appendix at the back of this book to see this in full. Ignore inverse characters if they appear, for they are not worth anything because they've been affected by solar radiation and mutated to their inverse form. The keys 5 and 8 steer you left and right in the direction of the arrows on the keys. You score when the debris is directly ahead of you on the screen and you "crash" into it.

Here is the program listing:

```
10 LET X=10
20 LET Y=10
30 LET S=0
40 LET F=5
50 LET F=F+1
60 PRINT AT 20,INT (RND*20);CH
R$ (INT (RND*63+1)+(128 AND RND<
.2));AT Y,X;" "
70 SCROLL
80 LET X=X+(INKEY$="8" AND X<1
9)-(INKEY$="5" AND X>0)
90 PRINT AT Y,X;"V";AT Y+1,X;
100 LET P=PEEK (PEEK 16398+256*
PEEK 16399)
110 IF P<64 THEN LET S=S+P
120 IF F<100 THEN GOTO 50
130 PRINT S
```

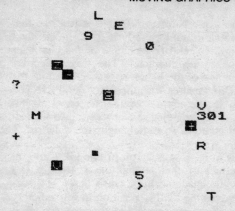

The position of your spaceship on screen is set by X (horizontal position) and Y (vertical position). These are initially set by lines 1Ø and 2Ø to a position at about the middle of the playing area of the screen. The variable S records your score and is set to 0 at the start of the game by line 3Ø. F is the variable that controls the duration of the game—it does not count in any particular unit but is a convenient way of controlling the duration of the game. The time is clocked up in line 5Ø, one unit of space-time at a time. The statement LET F=F+1 may confuse you a little since it is hard to imagine F being equal to F+1. It actually means add 1 to the old value of F to make the new value. Line 6Ø is rather complicated. It determines where the character is PRINTed, which character is PRINTed, and whether it's an inverse character. Let us look at the position first. The character is placed at the bottom of the playing area (the Y coordinate is set at 20 and the X coordinate to a value of from 0 to 19 by the random number expression). The expression after the semicolon generates a character at random from the number generated in parentheses after CHR8. The number generated is a random number from 1 to 63. The following expression may look rather strange, but all it does is determine whether to add 0 or 128 to this number (i.e., it determines whether the character generated is inverse or not). It is a special use of the function AND.

It looks at the following expression and adds 0 to the value if it is not true or the value before AND if it is true, so that 128 is added to the random number only if RND is less than 0.2, making it a roughly one-in-five chance of the character being an inverse, nonscoring character. The statement after this erases the old position of the V before it is scrolled up the screen by line 7Ø. This ensures that the V is not PRINTed anywhere other than in the middle of the screen. Line 8Ø checks the keyboard to see whether you're steering to the left or right or keeping it stationary, and changes the value of X accordingly.

The V is PRINTed in its new position in line 9Ø. Can you see now how the effect of this is that the spaceship (V) remains stationary while space seems to rush past? The second part of line 9Ø moves the PRINT position to immediately precede the position of the spaceship, so that we may find what is immediately in front of the spaceship by means of line 1ØØ, which finds the CODE of the character stored at that memory location by PEEKing the address held in the system variables 16398 and 16399. Line 11Ø checks to see if this character ahead of the spaceship is a scoring character (i.e., it has a CODE of less than 64, rather than less than 128 as you might expect from an inverse character detector, because this would permit CHR$ 118 ENTER markers that SCROLL might push up the screen).

You may want to add this line to the program to stop it if you hit a radiation-mutated piece of debris:

```
115 IF P>127 THEN GOTO 130
```

Here, we need to specify >127 to again exclude NEWLINE markers from fouling things up. If the character below the spaceship is a scoring character, then its CODE is added to your score in line 11Ø. Line 12Ø checks to see if your time is up (or your fuel has run out), then either PRINTs your score in line 13Ø if it is up or sends the program back for more action if you still have time left.

This program has dealt with the main details of moving graphics on your computer. There are three points to consider, however.

When PRINTing variables, the computer stores numbers in one format, then needs to change this to another format before they are printed. This takes quite a while, and slows

down moving graphics considerably. Try adding this line to
the UFO program:

```
105 PRINT AT 4,16;H
```

It was possible to PRINT variable H in the same program
because it was PRINTed at a time when there were no
moving graphics and therefore the delay was not noticed.

Also note that if you're PEEKing or POKEing into the
display file area of memory, you should bear in mind that if
there is more than 3¼K of memory plugged in, the screen is
automatically padded with spaces. The display is therefore
permanently at its full size unless you are using SCROLL,
which can introduce short lines.

When I say 3¼K, I should say when RAMTOP tells the
computer there is 3¼K of memory. RAMTOP is the name
given to the measurement the computer makes of the amount
of memory available for you to use for programs. If the computer is told by the value of RAMTOP that there is more
than 3¼K available, and you clear the screen, then the whole
screen is filled with spaces, or—in other words—the display
file is at its maximum size.

Assuming the display file is full size, you know the column
and line number for a PRINT AT command, and you wish to
find out its address in the display file before PRINTing for
any reason, you can do this in one of two ways. Suppose the
line and column number are Y and X, where Y tells us the
number of lines down the screen and X the number of columns across the screen. First, we can use the formula
PEEK (PEEK 16396 + 256*PEEK 16397 + 1 + Y*33 + X) to
tell us the CODE of the character at location Y,X. It
is also possible to use POKE (PEEK 16396 + 256*PEEK
16397 + Y*33 + X + 1) to place a character on screen at
location Y,X but this is the same as PRINT AT Y,X;
(this was used quite often on the 4K ROM ZX80 which
had no PRINT AT function but is not required on your
computer). Remember that this only works when the display
file is at full size. 16396 and 16397 are the system variables that contain the address of the start of the display
file.

The second method is the method used in the preceding
programs. The PRINT position is moved using PRINT AT Y,X;

to screen location Y,X. Using the expression PEEK (PEEK 16398 + 256*PEEK 16399), we can find the CODE of the character already at location Y,X. This second method is generally preferred because the display file does not have to be any particular size. The first method is only useful where we do not wish to move the PRINT position. (PEEK and POKE are covered in detail a little later.)

Finally, there is one other method of producing moving graphics in BASIC which is not used very often—through the use of strings. Strings may be PRINTed very rapidly, and the computer's comprehensive string slicing facilities (discussed earlier in the book) mean that we have at our disposal a powerful tool. The basic method is to assign a character or string array large enough to cover the area of screen used for movement and PRINT the array at a certain location. To simulate movement we can either PRINT different parts of the array or change the contents of the array.

PRINT different parts of the string in order by running this short program:

```
10 DIM A$(32)
20 LET A$(1)="+"
30 FOR A=32 TO 1 STEP -1
40 PRINT AT 20,0;A$(A TO )+A$(
TO A-1)
50 NEXT A
60 GOTO 30
```

Can you see why it is necessary to have line 30 count *backwards* from 31 to 1? What would happen if line 30 counted from 1 to 32 (30 FOR A=1 to 32)? Draw out on a piece of paper (or use the printer if you have one) every step that the program will take to make up the display. Note the high speed possible, and how the previous position is erased and the new position PRINTed in one go. An interesting effect may be obtained by changing line 20 to 20 INPUT A$ and entering a message of up to 32 characters. This is similar to a type of display found in shop windows for advertising purposes, although this is not the kind of effect one would normally encounter.

This method of producing moving graphics from strings is very useful because it does not alter the contents of strings/ arrays, but rather only displays them in a different order, so the information may be retrieved easily at any time. It can be used for a shop window display like the one below.

```
10 PRINT "ENTER MESSAGE"
20 INPUT A$
30 IF A$="" THEN GOTO 20
40 LET S=10
50 CLS
60 FOR B=1 TO LEN A$+33
70 PRINT AT 5,0;("                  "+A$+"                  ")(B TO B+31)
80 LET S=S-(2 AND INKEY$="F" AND S>1)+(2 AND INKEY$="D")
90 IF INKEY$="A" THEN PAUSE 4E4
100 FOR A=1 TO S
110 NEXT A
120 NEXT B
130 GOTO 60
```

What it does is ask you to enter a display message; after it has been entered, the message begins appearing from the right of the screen, and moving to the left and eventually disappearing to the left, whereupon the sequence begins all over again. The rotating sequence starts at a slow speed but can be speeded up by pressing the F key (the key with FAST written on it) or slowed down by pressing the D key (the key with SLOW written on it). The fastest speed is not very fast but is satisfactory. The slowest is very, very slow. You can "freeze" the display by pressing the A key (it has STOP written on it!) and it may be "unfrozen" by pressing any key except BREAK, whereupon the whole sequence continues from where it was stopped. You can stop the program at any time by pressing BREAK.

In theory, provided that the computer has enough memory available, the size of the message is limited by the size of the largest array the computer can handle. In practice, however, if you fill the screen with the message when entering it (i.e., it is more than 24 rows of 32 characters long), any subsequent characters entered have to be entered blind because they will seem to be below the screen. Try this to see what I mean. Warning: You'll end up with a tired finger!

The message begins to appear from the right of the screen about a quarter of the way down, and runs along the screen toward the left. Once it has disappeared past the left-hand side of the screen, it reappears as before and repeats the cycle over and over again. The speed may be varied as described. The display is frozen, but since the freeze routine uses PAUSE, there will be a "judder" or "flicker" of the display as it freezes. This may be remedied by adding the following lines to the program:

```
 90 IF INKEY$="A" THEN GOSUB 14
0
140 IF INKEY$<>"" THEN GOTO 140
150 IF INKEY$="" THEN GOTO 50
160 IF INKEY$<>"" THEN GOTO 160
170 RETURN
```

The subroutine at line 140 replaces PAUSE 4E4. Line 160 is necessary so that the program does not "unfreeze" until you let go of the unfreeze key and the routine does not retrigger when it gets to line 90. If you are uncertain of the function of all these new lines, try leaving one out to see what effect it has.

The only real point to note is that it is unwise to use keywords which are composed of more than one character (e.g., AND, TO, PRINT, etc.) since they will cause an overspill into the next line of the display, although they will clear themselves as the program proceeds because of the trailing space PRINTed when keywords are PRINTed.

Line 70 is fairly complex: To prevent changing the contents of string A$, the entire contents in the first pair of parentheses are treated as one long string consisting of 32 spaces followed by the message string A$, followed in turn by another 32 spaces. The slicer in the second pair of parentheses selects which parts of this long string are PRINTed. Note that A$ still retains its own identity. Whichever parts are selected, the string PRINTed is always 32 characters long.

As it stands, the program has no facility for you to change the message once it is running—you have to use BREAK and then RUN the program once again. One way of providing this facility is to add this line, so that on pressing "1" (EDIT) the program restarts automatically:

```
85 IF INKEY$="1" THEN GOTO 10
```

Move the elements of the array around. Try this program:

```
10 DIM A$(32)
20 FOR A=1 TO 32
30 LET A$(A)="+"
40 PRINT AT 20,0;A$
50 LET A$(A)=" "
60 NEXT A
70 GOTO 20
```

This method gives us great flexibility. We can handle strings quickly and efficiently with the computer's string-handling facilities. Strings are very useful for storing information; this information may be accessed quickly and conveniently as compared to REM statements, for example, and the speed with which strings may be PRINTed makes them an attractive method for producing displays. The main disadvantage is that they are wasteful of memory since the information is held in both the display file and the arrays involved, and possibly in the program area as well. Here is a moving display program which relies on information in the strings PRINTed.

BASIC Invaders

The program is called BASIC Invaders because it's a version of the arcade game written in BASIC. It is very simplified of necessity and is included for the purpose of demonstrating the use of strings for moving display purposes. A row of invaders (inverse +) descends the screen toward you (inverse A). You can move left or right using the 5 and 8 keys respectively. You fire up at the invaders by pressing the 7 key. If you are directly under an invader, it disappears and is destroyed. However, if you fire when there is no invader above, then a new invader appears to penalize you. There are seven waves of invaders, and you have to destroy them all to win.

```
 1 REM --BASIC INVADERS--
10 DIM A$(32)
20 DIM B$(32)
30 FOR D=1 TO 7
40 LET A$=" +    +    +    +    +
 +    +    "
50 LET X=INT (RND*32)
60 LET C=X
70 PRINT AT 5,0;"WAVE:";D
80 LET C=0
90 FOR B=D+9 TO 19 STEP 2
```

```
100 FOR A=0 TO 31
110 LET X=X+(INKEY$="8" AND X<3
1)-(INKEY$="5" AND X>0)
120 PRINT AT B,0;A$;AT 20,C;" "
AND C<>X;AT 20,X;"A"
130 IF A$=B$ THEN GOTO 200+(60
AND D=7)
140 LET C=X
150 IF INKEY$="7" THEN LET A$(X
+1)=CHR$ (21 AND A$(X+1)=" ")
160 NEXT A
170 PRINT AT B,0;B$
180 NEXT B
190 GOTO 240
200 FOR B=1 TO 50
210 NEXT B
220 PRINT AT 20,C;" "
230 NEXT D
240 PRINT "OOPS...THEY LANDED"
250 STOP
260 PRINT "ALL DESTROYED"
```

The program is very wasteful of memory. No attempt has
been made to conserve memory, and you may be able to
speed it up with some minor modifications. The two strings
of interest are A$ and B$. B$ is merely set up to 32 spaces and
is used to prevent typing in "(32 spaces)" at various points in
the program. A$ is the string that represents the invaders. It is
initially set to 32 elements, the number of characters in one
line of display. Line 40 sets the initial state of the characters
and can be any combination of spaces and + and should
consist of 32 characters. X is the variable that controls your
position and its value is altered in line 110. Line 120 performs
the main PRINTing, updating the invaders display and your
position.

Line 130 compares the invaders with a string of 32 spaces
(B$), and if it finds that A$ contains no invaders (i.e., it is all
spaces), it either causes a jump to the next wave of invaders
or, if you're already on the last wave, it causes a jump to the
victory message at line 260. Line 150 is of particular interest,
since it scans the string for the character above you in the
invader display, and if it finds a + there, it converts it to a
space, or vice versa. This is only done if the 7 key is pressed.

The rest of the program is mainly concerned with timing of
loops, sorting out the different waves of invaders. Line 100
controls the rate at which the invaders descend down the

screen. This may be altered to provide a handicap facility if you like. As it stands, the program tends to speed up (deliberately) as the game goes on by means of the D/3 in line 100. Again, change this if you like, to achieve a different effect. An alternative is to add

```
   2 PRINT "ENTER SKILL LEVEL (3
0 - 100)"
   3 INPUT E
   4 IF E<30 OR E>100 THEN GOTO
3
 100 FOR A=0 TO E
```

If you're storing the entire screen in a string array (or a part of the screen involving lines above or below each other), then you can utilize two different methods using different types of array. Consider the case of the full 22-by-32 screen. You will require a 22- by 32-element string array, and this may be accomplished by either one of these methods:

1. Using a two-dimensional array, set up with the statement DIM A$(22,32). You can then use the PRINT AT coordinates to access the elements, remembering that the array elements start with 1, and PRINT coordinates with 0. For example, to PRINT AT Y,X;CHR$ T you would say LET A$(Y+1,X+1)=CHR$ T. The problem with this method is that a lengthy PRINT statement is required to place the entire array on the screen, i.e., PRINT AT 0,0;A$(1), A$(2),A$(3) . . . A$(21), A$(22). However, since the main reason for using an array for printing is the ease of access of information, this is only necessary at the very beginning of a program since from then on we need only PRINT the parts of the array we're actually dealing with. Take the example of a game of checkers. We would need the entire board on screen at the start of the game, and we must be able to examine the board in its entirety; however, when it comes to PRINTing moves, we need only PRINT the parts of the array which are changed by a move—the part of the array from which the piece was moved, the part to which it is moved, and possibly a part of the array where an opposing piece was captured.

2. Use a single-dimension array with 704 elements for the 22-by-32 display, set up by the statement DIM A$(704).

This can be treated like a memory-mapped screen PRINTed in one go by the statement PRINT AT Ø;Ø;A$ and which is very fast to execute. The elements are easily accessed. To move a character on screen we have to move it about in the array in a manner which makes it move satisfactorily on screen. To understand how to do this we have to understand the layout of the array on the screen. Here is a diagram:

X Y	Ø	1	2	29	3Ø	31
Ø	A$(1)	A$(2)	A$(3)	A$(3Ø)	A$(31)	A$(32)
1	A$(33)	A$(34)	A$(35)	A$(62)	A$(63)	A$(64)
2	A$(65)	A$(66)	A$(67)	A$(94)	A$(95)	A$(96)
3	A$(97)	A$(98)	A$(99)	A$(126)	A$(127)	A$(128)

The diagram shows a fragment from the top of the screen. Y and X are the coordinates of the PRINT AT Y,X; function. Can you see how the Y,X; coordinates can be related to the subscripts of A$? There are 32 elements of A$ in each line of the display. The X coordinates start off at Ø, whereas the array subscripts start at 1. So Y,X corresponds to A$(Y*32 + X + 1). When a character is moved, it can go to one of eight locations all around it, as shown in the diagram below:

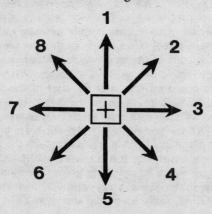

Now suppose the + is at A$(A). Here is a chart showing how much the difference is between subscripts of the elements representing the possible positions on all sides (how much to add to the old subscript to make it the new one).

DIRECTION OF MOVEMENT	HOW MUCH TO ADD TO A
1	−32
2	−31
3	1
4	33
5	32
6	31
7	−1
8	−33

At this stage we have to be careful not to go beyond the limits of the array, as we would when using PRINT, to avoid crashing the program with a subscript error. We can use the cursor keys to control vertical movement and horizontal movement, and use the SHIFTed cursor keys for diagonal movement. To illustrate how this may be done, here is a short program which moves a + around the screen under cursor control.

Pressing shift-5, shift-6, shift-7, and shift-8 moves you 45° clockwise in the direction of the arrows on the keys. The 5, 6, 7, and 8 keys by themselves cause movement in the direction of the arrows. This program does not have the facility to prevent subscript errors occurring because of characters that are moved outside the boundaries of the array.

```
10 DIM A$(704)
20 LET A=INT (RND*704)+1
30 LET A$(A)=" "
40 LET A=A-(32 AND INKEY$="7")
-(31 AND INKEY$=CHR$ 112)+(1 AND
 INKEY$="8")+(33 AND INKEY$=CHR$
 115)+(32 AND INKEY$="6")+(31 AN
D INKEY$=CHR$ 113)-(1 AND INKEY$
="5")-(33 AND INKEY$=CHR$ 114)
50 LET A$(A)="+"
60 PRINT AT 0,0;A$
70 GOTO 30
```

The reason that shift-5, shift-6, shift-7, and shift-8 have been represented by CHR$ 114, CHR$ 113, CHR$ 112, and CHR$ 115 is that they cannot be entered directly from the keyboard (they act as cursor controls if you try), so the easiest way to get them in is by means of CHR$.

It should be emphasized that the use of strings to create moving graphics is limited to those applications where speed is not of great importance. It is very useful in applications where the access of information is important, but speed of graphics is not of highest priority; an example is a board game such as checkers, where pieces move occasionally but rapid access to information is not necessary.

CHAPTER 14
Introduction to arithmetic
on the computer

Have a quick glance at· this section before you read it in detail. You may well find it has no new information for you. If this is the case, feel free to turn to the next section.

The symbols for the various operations in BASIC are probably well known to you by now. They are multiply (*), divide (/), subtract (−), add (+), raise to the power (* * − shift-H). The computer follows a strict priority for operations.

The term *priority* refers to the order in which expressions are evaluated. The computer does not necessarily evaluate things in the order in which they are printed on the screen. For example, you may have noticed that putting an expression in parentheses could produce a different result compared with the same expression evaluated with the parentheses omitted (indeed, leaving out parentheses may cause the computer to give you a syntax error). We formalize this by giving each operation a *priority*, a number between 1 and 16.

The operations with highest priority are evaluated first, and operations with equal priority are evaluated in order from left to right. In effect, the computer looks at the expression and finds the part with the highest priority, and "says": "Wait a minute, fellers, there's something with a higher priority than you over there—I'll come back to you in a minute when it's your turn."

Here is a list of various operations and their priorities:

Operation	Priority
()	16
SUBSCRIPTING/SLICING	12
ALL FUNCTIONS	11
**	10
− (negation)	9
*	8
/	8
+	6
− (subtraction)	6
=,>,<,<=,>=,<>	5
NOT	4
AND	3
OR	2

Note that a number is assumed to be positive unless it is preceded by a minus sign. Similarly, unless a decimal point appears within a number, the computer will assume it is an integer. Although you can use decimal points when working with the computer, commas are not allowed. The use of *scientific notation* for very large and very small numbers was explained in the section on variables. Refer back to that section if you need a reminder on how this works.

Compared with the time it would take you to work out a calculation using a pen and paper, the computer works very quickly, as can be seen by running the following arithmetic programs. The first program in this section works out arithmetic progressions. You must enter the first term, the common difference, and the number of terms, and the computer will produce the information for you very rapidly.

```
10 REM ARITHMETIC PROGRESSION
20 PRINT "I WILL WORK OUT FOR
YOU THE"
30 PRINT "ARITHMETIC PROGRESSI
ON FROM THE"
40 PRINT "INFORMATION YOU GIVE
ME"
45 PRINT
50 PRINT "ENTER THE FIRST TERM
"
60 INPUT FIRST
70 PRINT ,FIRST
```

```
  80 PRINT "AND THE COMMON DIFFE
RENCE?"
  90 INPUT DIFF
 100 PRINT ,DIFF
 110 PRINT "HOW MANY TERMS?"
 120 INPUT TERMS
 130 LET TERMS=INT (TERMS+.5)
 140 CLS
 150 SCROLL
 160 PRINT "ARITHMETIC PROGRESSI
ON"
 170 SCROLL
 180 PRINT "TERM NUMBER";TAB 13;
"VALUE"
 190 LET COUNT=0
 200 FOR L=0 TO TERMS-1
 210 LET W=L+1
 220 LET Q=FIRST+(L*DIFF)
 230 LET COUNT=COUNT+Q
 235 SCROLL
 240 PRINT TAB 4;W;TAB 13;Q
 250 NEXT L
 260 SCROLL
 270 PRINT TAB 4;"THE SUM IS ";C
OUNT
```

```
I WILL WORK OUT FOR YOU THE
ARITHMETIC PROGRESSION FROM THE
INFORMATION YOU GIVE ME

ENTER THE FIRST TERM
                66
AND THE COMMON DIFFERENCE?
                3
HOW MANY TERMS?

ARITHMETIC PROGRESSION
TERM NUMBER    VALUE
       1          66
       2          69
       3          72
       4          75
       5          78
       6          81
       7          84
       8          87
       9          90
      10          93
      11          96
      12          99
     THE SUM IS 990
```

As you can see, the program also works out the sum of the terms:

```
I WILL WORK OUT FOR YOU THE
ARITHMETIC PROGRESSION FROM THE
INFORMATION YOU GIVE ME

ENTER THE FIRST TERM
                .0034
AND THE COMMON DIFFERENCE?
                .00012
HOW MANY TERMS?
                6


ARITHMETIC PROGRESSION
TERM NUMBER    VALUE
     1        .0034
     2        .00352
     3        .00364
     4        .00376
     5        .00388
     6        .004
     THE SUM IS .0222
```

Prime numbers are very easy to determine:

```
  10 REM ** PRIME NUMBER **
  20 PRINT "ENTER THE VALUE OF T
HE"
  30 PRINT " MAXIMUM PRIME NUMBE
R"
  40 PRINT TAB 4;"THAT YOU WANT"
  50 INPUT A
  60 DIM Z(A)
  70 FOR J=1 TO A
  75 LET Z(J) =J
  80 NEXT J
  85 IF A<4 THEN GOTO 200
  90 LET Z(4) =5
  95 LET KL=4
 100 LET IZ=5
 110 LET IZ=IZ+2
 120 IF IZ>A THEN GOTO 200
 125 LET JO=2
 130 LET EX=IZ/Z(JO+1)
 140 IF EX=INT (EX) THEN GOTO 11
0
 150 IF EX<Z(JO+1) THEN GOTO 180
 160 LET JO=JO+1
 170 GOTO 130
 180 LET KL=KL+1
```

```
185 LET Z(KL)=IZ
190 GOTO 110
200 CLS
220 PRINT "THE PRIME NUMBERS UP
TO ";A
230 PRINT TAB 4;"PRIME NO.","PR
IME"
240 FOR C=1 TO KL
250 PRINT TAB 4;C,Z(C)
260 IF 16*INT (C/16)=C THEN INP
UT U$
270 IF 16*INT (C/16)=C THEN CLS
280 NEXT C
```

The mathematical ability of the computer can also, of course, be turned to produce other kinds of information.

This next program, a series of statistical routines, can easily be broken down into four shorter programs, by entering the line numbers from 1000 to 1500, 2000 to 2510, 3000 to 3510 *or* 4000 to 4100. You'll also have to assign COUNT and TOTAL for each program.

The four programs are:

Arithmetic mean, which is simply the average of a set of numbers.

Geometric mean, which is the nth root of the product of the numbers, where n is the total number of numbers entered.

Harmonic mean, which takes the reciprocal of the arithmetic mean of the reciprocals of the numbers entered.

Factorial, which is the progression $A*(A-1)*(A-2)*(A-3)$ ... down to $*(2)*(1)$, where A is the integer entered in line 4030. As this only works with integers, line 4040 changes any noninteger entry into an integer.

The routine from line 9000 presents a menu of choices. Note the use of GOTO A*1000 in line 9600. This is a short way of saying

IF A = 1 THEN GOTO 1000
IF A = 2 THEN GOTO 2000
IF A = 3 THEN GOTO 3000
IF A = 4 THEN GOTO 4000

You can often make use of this technique in menu-driven programs.

```
  10 REM STATISTICAL PROGRAMS
  20 REM BY KEN MAHOGANY
  30 GOTO 9000
1000 REM ARITHMETIC MEAN
1010 PRINT "ARITHMETIC MEAN"
1020 PRINT "ENTER THE NUMBERS YO
U WISH ME"
1030 PRINT TAB 5;"TO AVERAGE FOR
 YOU"
1040 PRINT "ENTER E TO END YOUR
INPUT"
1060 INPUT Q$
1070 IF Q$="E" THEN GOTO 1400
1080 PRINT Q$;"   ";
1090 LET TOTAL=TOTAL+VAL (Q$)
1100 LET COUNT=COUNT+1
1110 GOTO 1060
1400 PRINT
1410 PRINT
1500 PRINT "THE ARITHMETIC MEAN
IS ";TOTAL/COUNT
1510 GOTO 9000
2000 REM GEOMETRIC MEAN
2010 PRINT "GEOMETRIC MEAN"
2020 PRINT "ENTER THE NUMBERS YO
U WISH ME"
2030 PRINT "TO USE TO FIND GEOME
TRIC MEAN"
2040 PRINT "ENTER E TO END YOUR
INPUT"
2050 LET TOTAL=1
2060 INPUT Q$
2070 IF Q$="E" THEN GOTO 2500
2075 PRINT Q$;"   ";
2080 LET COUNT=COUNT+1
2090 LET TOTAL=TOTAL*VAL Q$
2100 GOTO 2060
2500 PRINT
2510 PRINT "THE GEOMETRIC MEAN I
S ";TOTAL**(1/COUNT)
2520 GOTO 9000
3000 REM HARMONIC MEAN
3010 PRINT "HARMONIC MEAN"
3020 PRINT "ENTER THE NUMBERS YO
U WISH ME"
3030 PRINT "TO USE TO FIND HARMO
NIC MEAN"
3040 PRINT "ENTER E TO END YOUR
INPUT"
3050 INPUT Q$
3060 IF Q$="E" THEN GOTO 3500
3080 PRINT Q$;"   ";
3090 LET TOTAL=TOTAL+(1/VAL Q$)
```

```
3100 LET COUNT=COUNT+1
3110 GOTO 3050
3500 PRINT
3510 PRINT "THE HARMONIC MEAN IS
     ";1/(TOTAL/COUNT)
3520 GOTO 9000
4000 REM FACTORIAL
4010 PRINT "FACTORIAL"
4020 PRINT "ENTER AN INTEGER"
4030 INPUT NUM
4040 LET NUM=INT (NUM)
4050 LET A=1
4060 FOR B=1 TO NUM
4070 LET A=A*B
4080 NEXT B
4090 PRINT
4100 PRINT "THE FACTORIAL OF ";N
UM;" IS ";A
4110 GOTO 9000
8990 STOP
9000 PRINT
9005 PRINT "SELECT THE PROGRAM Y
OU WANT"
9010 PRINT "1 - ARITHMETIC MEAN"
9020 PRINT "2 - GEOMETRIC MEAN"
9030 PRINT "3 - HARMONIC MEAN"
9040 PRINT "4 - FACTORIAL"
9045 PRINT ,"5 TO END"
9050 INPUT A
9060 IF A<1 OR A>5 THEN GOTO 905
0
9062 IF A=5 THEN STOP
9065 CLS
9500 LET TOTAL=0
9510 LET COUNT=0
9520 PRINT
9600 GOTO A*1000
```

The final program in this section uses the computer to simulate the life cycles of two species, one of which preys upon the other, and to graph their relative populations. The relationship between the two species is controlled by a differential equation. You enter the starting populations as numbers between 1 and 5. Fractions are acceptable, and it is fascinating to enter a very low population for one of the animals and a high one for the other, and watch the two evolve. When the program has run through a specified number of generations, it will stop. This is so you can enter another starting population for the first species. Press ENTER, and you can now enter the starting level of the second species. The development of this relationship will then be graphed, on top of the existing graph, so you can build up a number of graphs showing the effects of different starting populations for the predator and its prey.

```
10 REM SPECIES
20 PRINT "HOW MANY OF SPECIES
ONE?"
30 INPUT X
40 PRINT "AND OF SPECIES TWO?"
50 INPUT Y
55 CLS
60 FOR Z=1 TO 20
70 FOR T=1 TO 7 STEP .5
80 PRINT AT 1,1; INT (X*10000);
" "
90 PRINT AT 2,1; INT (Y*10000);
" "
100 LET X=X+(4*X-2*X*Y)*0.01
110 LET Y=Y+(X*Y-3*Y)*0.01
120 PLOT 6*X,6*Y
130 NEXT T
140 NEXT Z
150 INPUT X
160 INPUT Y
170 GOTO 60
```

Functions

The computer's dialect of BASIC, like other BASICs, contains a number of preprogrammed functions which you can use in a program, or in the direct mode. The following discussion includes a program which uses a *defined function* to draw a picture of a bat!

General functions are as follows:

ABS This function, ABSolute, gives the value of X, ignoring the sign, so that if X is –10, ABS(X) would be 10. Similarly, if X is 10, ABS(X) is still 10.

INT The INT function gives the whole number, or INTeger part of a number, giving the largest number which is not greater than X. If X is 2.42, INT(X) would be 2.

INT rounds off numbers to the next lowest whole number, e.g., INT 2.2 is 2, INT 2.9 is 2, INT 2 is 2, and so on. A frequent requirement is to round off numbers to the nearest whole number, so that 2.6 becomes 3, etc. (Some commands do this automatically, e.g., PRINT AT, POKE.) This is quite easy to do. Suppose the number to be rounded off is A. If we first add 0.5 to A and then apply INT, the answer will be the nearest whole number. If, as an example, A was 2.6 and we wished to round off to the nearest whole number, PRINT INT (2.6 + 0.5) would give 3, whereas PRINT INT (2.3 + 0.5) would give 2. PRINT INT (2.5 + 0.5) is rounded up to 3.

It is often necessary, when carrying out calculations with money, to have answers to two decimal places, to resemble dollars and cents. The following routine does this, adds the dollar sign, and lines up the numbers with the decimal points underneath each other. You might like to try adding a version of this to the compound and simple interest program given earlier in the book.

```
10 INPUT A
20 LET A$=STR$ (INT (A*100+0.5
)/100)
25 IF A$(1)="." THEN LET A$="0
"+A$
30 LET B=LEN A$-LEN STR$ INT V
AL A$
40 LET A$=A$+(".00" AND B=0)+(
"0" AND B=2)
50 PRINT TAB 10-LEN STR$ INT V
AL A$;"$";A$
60 GOTO 10
```

```
$444.00
 $88.70
 $98.50
  $0.05
$44.54
  $0.09
 $4.00
 $4.30
```

```
10 INPUT A
20 LET A$=STR$ (INT (A*100+0.5
)/100)
25 IF A$(1)="." THEN LET A$="0
"+A$
30 LET B=LEN A$-LEN STR$ INT V
AL A$
40 LET A$=A$+(".00" AND B=0)+(
"0" AND B=2)
50 PRINT "£";A$
60 GOTO 10
```

RND This is used to generate a RaNDom number. RND gives a random number between 0 and 1.

SGN This function returns the SiGN of the variable in parentheses, the SiGN of the *argument* as this variable is known. If X equals 20, that is, X is a positive number, then SGN(X) = 1, SGN(−20) = −1, and SGN(0) = 0.

TAB As pointed out earlier in the book, this is the TABulating function, which moves the PRINT position across the line the number of spaces indicated by the argument of the function. Thus, PRINT TAB(6);"$" will print the $ at the seventh position across from the left-hand edge, while PRINT TAB(13);"$" will print it 14 spaces across. The direction down and across the screen can be specified, as was pointed out earlier, by using PRINT AT. Thus PRINT AT 4,9,"$" will print a dollar sign on the fifth line down, in the tenth position across. TAB reduces a number modulo 32, meaning that the argument of (number after) TAB can be larger than 31; it will be reduced to a number in the range 0 to 31, and the PRINT position moves on the same line unless this would involve backspacing, in which case it moves on to the next line. Modulo means that the argument of TAB is divided by 32 (the number of columns per line on a screen) and the remainder taken. You may be able to take advantage of this when the PRINT spacing is determined by calculation since you do not have to ensure that the number falls in the range from 0 to 31.

EXP This function gives the value of e (the constant which governs exponential change, approximately equal to 2.718, which you can see by asking the T/S 1000 to PRINT EXP 1) raised to the power of the argument, so PRINT EXP 5 will give 148.41316.

LN LN X yields the natural logarithm to base e, so PRINT LN 5 gives 1.6094379.

SQR This function yields the SQuare Root of a number, so when X is 5, PRINT SQR X gives 2.236068.

Here is a listing of trigonometric functions:

SIN This gives the sine of an angle in radians. SIN 5 yields −0.95892428.

COS Yields the cosine of an angle in radians. PRINT COS X where X equals 5 gives 0.28366219.

TAN Produces the tangent of angle X in radians. (The computer measures angles in radians. PI radians equals 180°.)

CHAPTER 15
PEEK and POKE

These two commands are very powerful instructions that enable you to do things with your computer that you might not be able to do otherwise. Let us start by defining the two terms:

1. PEEK m gives us the number stored at address m in memory.
2. POKE m,n puts number n into memory at address m. When the number is accepted, it erases what used to be there.

The term ADDRESS needs explaining. A computer like yours thinks and remembers in numbers, not in words as people do. Certain patterns of numbers make certain parts of the computer do certain things. This is called a *program*. The computer needs a way to hold all these numbers so that they are remembered and can be looked at when needed. Once the computer knows their values and patterns, it can decide what it's going to do.

Certain patterns of numbers may make the computer PRINT something on the screen, add two numbers together, or crash if the pattern of numbers makes it try to do something it can't or shouldn't. The computer can't just place the numbers anywhere—this would cause chaos if it didn't know where to look next. So there is a method used whereby everything can be neatly organized.

Imagine that you wanted to display a message in public, and you had the words written on little placards with hooks on them, ready for all occurrences, so that you could display any message simply by hanging up the right set of placards.

For example, if we wanted to display this message: "BE-WARE ROAD WORKS," we need the placards

BEWARE   ROAD   and   WORKS

We also need a board on which to hang up these words. If we start with the first hook by hanging the first placard there and proceed along the board, we end up with a fairly neat sign:

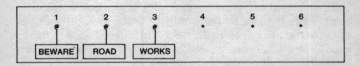

The pegs on the board tell us where each word is hanging. This can be compared to your computer's memory. There are 65535 places where we can "hang" numbers on the T/S, but these are split up for various uses, and you or the computer can do various things with these. These "pegs," or locations, or whatever you want to call them are actually referred to as *addresses* (the home of each number, if you like). However, if the T/S has a number it wants to store, it can't just place it anywhere because it might upset what's already there. Let us now look at the addresses and how they are laid out.

ROM	Unused	1K RAM inside the ZX81	SINCLAIR 16K RAMPACK if fitted	Not normally used
Ø	8192	16384	17408	32768	65536

The first part, called ROM, is rather special. It is a set of instructions that tells the computer how to do various functions and can translate or interpret the lines of BASIC you enter as parts of a program into numbers that mean something to your computer. ROM means *read-only memory*, because its contents are fixed and cannot easily be altered without destroying it. You can look into it as you like, and this is often very useful.

The second part is unused on your computer, although a little design trick makes it look like a copy of the ROM. This part is of little interest to us.

The part which is of most interest starts at 16384. This part is called RAM, short for random access memory. Like its name suggests, you can do anything to any part of this—you can read the values contained in any address or put a new value into any address.

To return to our previous example, if we look at the first peg (PEEK 1), we find the word BEWARE there. If we look at the second peg (PEEK 2), we find the word ROAD there, and so on. Can you see the analogy? Remember that the computer would use numbers rather than words, but the idea is still the same. Similarly, we can change the words on the pegs quite easily by using POKE to stuff a new number where another number used to be. We could do something like POKE peg 2, BUILDING, which would put the word BUILDING on the second peg of the notice, and thereby change its entire meaning. The great secret about PEEK and POKE is not what they do but how to use them. It's all very well finding what number is in which address or stuffing a new number into a particular address, but how can you make use of this in a program and how do you know where to PEEK and POKE? The answer is that you can do this mainly by experience and by reading through other people's programs, although you will find that as your knowledge of computers increases, you will find you think up new ways to use PEEK and POKE. Before we look at examples, let us briefly review how to write PEEK and POKE statements.

PEEK m. m is the address which we're looking into. m is a number from 0 to 65560 (e.g., PEEK 17000) or m can be the result of a calculation, provided it is a number in the range above, PEEK $(Y*33 + X + 1)$.

POKE m,n. m is an address to which the new number is to be placed, as with PEEK. It is written between the word POKE and the comma. The number after the comma, n, is the number to be placed in address m, and can be a number from 0 to 255 or the result of a calculation, provided it is a number from 0 to 255. You can actually make n a negative value from 0 to −255, but this is not very useful.

Let us now look at some examples of PEEK and POKE in use.

REM statements

Many programs rely on information held in REM statements in the first line of a BASIC program on the computer. This is because it is easy to access and is very economical on memory. The important point is that the address of the first character after the word REM in the first line of a program is 16514. So if you had the program

```
1 REM ABCDEF
2 PRINT PEEK 16514
```

it would print the number 38 on the screen. This is the CODE of the character A, so address 16514 has the value of 38. You can easily change this value by POKEing a new value into 16514. For example, to change A to a Z, look up the CODE of Z, which is 63, and POKE this into 16514:

```
POKE 16514,63
```

This can be written as POKE 16514, CODE "Z" which works just as well. The next address, 16515, stores the B, 16516 stores the C, and so on.

The technique of PEEKing/POKEing into REM statements is also of great importance with the storage of machine-code programs. This is an important, powerful programming technique and you are recommended to learn it if you do not already know about it.

Using the timer

The timer is contained in addresses 16436 and 16437, and, as you may recall, its use was discussed for timing player inputs. Note that the timer counts backwards, starting from 65536. Use these two statements to reset it:

```
POKE 16436,255
POKE 16437,255
```

And in order to read its value, we have to use this expression:

```
LET TIME=65536-PEEK 16436-256*PE
EK 16437
```

This gives us an answer in frames, and since 50 frames are sent to the TV every second, we need to divide by 50 to get an answer in seconds, as follows:

```
LET TIME=(65536-PEEK 16436-256*P
EEK 16437)/50
```

Here is a program to provide a stopwatch:

```
 10 POKE 16436,255
 20 POKE 16437,255
 30 PRINT AT 11,14; INT ((65536-
PEEK 16436-256*PEEK 16437)/50)
 40 GOTO 30
```

The INT in line 30 is added to prevent fractions of a second being printed. This stopwatch keeps fairly accurate time because the frame counter is controlled by special hardware, so unless the program deliberately forces it to do otherwise, it is independent of how fast the program runs and keeps time fairly well; even if the speed of the program only allows it to be read every 3 seconds. The counting range of the frame counter only allows timing for just under 11 minutes. If you want a readout in minutes and seconds, use this routine:

```
10 POKE 16436,255
20 POKE 16437,255
30 LET TIME=(65536-PEEK 16436-
256*PEEK 16437)/50
40 PRINT AT 11,12;INT (TIME/60
);":";INT (TIME-INT (TIME/60)*60
);" "
50 GOTO 30
```

This prints the minutes elapsed and seconds separated by a colon. A space is included at the end because, as the seconds clock from 59 to 0, a trailing digit may be left on the screen which could cause confusion in readings—leave the space out to see what I mean.

The 24-line screen

Normally, you can only PRINT on screen lines Ø to 21. There is a system variable called DF-SZ which contains the number of lines (including one blank line) in the lower part of the screen normally used for INPUT or error report codes. Its address is 16418 and its normal value is 2, but if we give it a value of 0, we can use PRINT AT to print on lines 22 and 23.

It is best not to use INPUT while 16418 has been altered or you may cause a system crash, so to restore the bottom of the screen to normal, POKE 16418,2 should be used before any INPUT statement. If 16418 has a value of less than 2, then SCROLL should not be used either. But if a number greater than 2 is POKEd into 16418, then SCROLL begins to operate from a different point than usual—a part screen scroll in BASIC! What is more, the PRINT position is moved to the line from which SCROLL operates!

PEEKing/POKEing into the display file

See the section on moving graphics for a detailed explanation.

Suppressing the error report codes

When you have a program where the display is very important (e.g., at an exhibition or in educational programs), it can be detracting or even embarrassing trying to explain "those funny little numbers at the bottom of the screen." Here is a method whereby you can prevent the error report code from appearing.

The error report code is determined by the value of address 16384, the first system variable. The trick is to POKE numbers into 16384 that do not cause anything to be printed or to print spaces which, of course, cannot be seen. These values may be POKEd into 16384 for this purpose: 43, 70, 72, 73, 74, 75, 76, 77, 79, 81, 82, 89.

Here is an example:

```
POKE 16384,74
```

You may find that certain numbers do not produce the desired result with certain programs. In this case, choose another number from the list. SAVE the program on tape before RUNning it if you're at all worried!

Great system crashes

Fun time again! Careless use of POKE can ruin programs by overwriting vital parts or can even cause a system crash where the computer appears to seize up, and nothing you do will make the computer do anything except switching it off.

Here are some of the exciting things you can do to your computer if you like abusing it!

1. Overwrite some of the ENTER characters, particularly in the display file—try this program:

```
10 LET P=PEEK 16396+256*PEEK 16397
20 POKE P,0
```

Now try to get a normal display! The screen appears to have gone haywire if you press ENTER after running the program. All it does is find the start of the display file in line 1Ø from the system variable 16396/16397 which has this specific purpose, and changes the character found normally at this location (an ENTER character CHR$ 118) to a space by using POKE. The poor machine then gets confused when trying to produce a listing.

2. For some novel displays, try POKEing all the numbers from 0 to 255 into the system variable 16384 that controls the error code.

3. Load your favorite program, add a line or two to reset the frame counter to 0, and wait for a while to see the result (the frame counter is system variable 16436/7 and is reset to 0 by POKE 16436,Ø and POKE 16437,Ø). It may not work every time, but is usually quite effective!

4. Try this program:

```
10 POKE 16418,0
20 INPUT A$
```

Where did the program go?

5. This is the classic POKE anything anywhere at random. RUN it several times to see the different effects possible.

```
10 POKE 16384+INT (RND*1024),INT (RND*1024)
20 GOTO 10
```

You may want to use the printer if you have one to keep a record of the interesting ones:

```
10 LET ADDRESS=16384+INT (RND*1024)
20 LET R=INT (RND*256)
30 LPRINT "ADDRESS=";ADDRESS
40 LPRINT "NUMBER TO POKE=";R
50 POKE ADDRESS,R
60 GOTO 10
```

Too much fun gets boring. Back to some more serious things.

Length of programs

Here is how the computer's RAM is organized:

PART OF RAM	HOW TO FIND THE ADDRESS OF THE BOUNDARIES
	16384
system variables	
	16509
program	
	PEEK 16395 + 256*16397
display file (screen picture)	
	PEEK 16400 + 256*PEEK 16401
variables	
byte with CHR$ 128	
	PEEK 16404 + 256*PEEK 16405
work space	
	PEEK 16410 + 256*PEEK 16411
calculator stack	
	PEEK 16412 + 256*PEEK 16413
space memory	
	Stack pointer— not accessible from BASIC
machine stack	
	PEEK 16386 + 256*PEEK 16387
GOSUB stack	
	PEEK 16388 + 256*PEEK 16389

The number of bytes used for the system variables is 125. To find how much memory is occupied by the program alone, excluding system variables and display, use this line:

```
PRINT PEEK 16396+256*PEEK 16397
-16509
```

This line will give the number of bytes occupied by the program, variables, system variables, and display:

```
PRINT PEEK 16404+256*PEEK 16405
-16384
```

This line gives the memory left for the user, perhaps the most useful one-line test of them all. It does not, however, take into account the stack (the area of memory which is reserved for the storage of data and such things as the return address from a GOSUB) because the stack pointer (a register which holds the address of the top of the stack) cannot be accessed from BASIC:

```
PRINT PEEK 16386+256*PEEK 16387
-PEEK 16412-256*PEEK 16413-81
```

Note that you need to subtract 81 because of the length of the statement.

Inserting noneditable lines into listings

Normally, if you have a title/author REM statement in a listing, it is fairly simple for others to delete these lines, thus denying you your authorship. However, you can make them impossible to remove by changing the line number of the first line of the program to Ø. The first line of a program is stored at address 16509, and the line number occupies two bytes. We can change these with POKE. The two bytes are stored so that the more significant byte is followed by the less significant byte (that is, the more important—highest—part is stored first, with the less important—lowest—part second).

Here is how to change a line number to Ø:

```
POKE 16509,0
POKE 16510,0
```

Now try to delete the first line. Quite secure, isn't it? The only way is to POKE a nonzero line number into 16509,10. So anybody who knew about the technique could easily delete the line.

A slightly better method is to change a line number in the middle of a listing. This is more difficult because we have no way of knowing where individual lines start. A starting point is the knowledge that program lines end with an ENTER character (CHR$ 118) and the next line will begin with the line number. Take this example:

```
10 REM VAT CALCULATOR
20 PRINT "ENTER AMOUNT LESS VA
T:";
30 INPUT A
40 REM (C) FRED BLOGGS 1982
50 PRINT A
60 PRINT "VAT=";A*15/100
```

We need to change line 40 to line 0 and keep it located in its present position in the listing to make it difficult to delete or edit. Using the information we have, add these lines to the program:

```
9000 FOR F=16509 TO PEEK 16396+2
56*PEEK 16397-3
9010 IF PEEK F=118 AND 256*PEEK
(F+1)+PEEK (F+2)=40 THEN GOTO 90
40
9020 NEXT F
9030 STOP
9040 POKE F+1,0
9050 POKE F+2,0
```

Now delete lines 9000 to 9050 and then try to delete line 0.

Incidentally, to make the program safer, it is normally better to insert this new line 0 at the point higher in a listing than line 255, since it will then be necessary to change two bytes of the listing to get rid of line 0. Another way to do the same thing is to use the system variable NXTLIN (16425/16426) to find the address of the start of the next line, provided you have space to add a few extra lines to the listing. We'll use this example:

```
10 REM PATTERNS
20 INPUT A$
30 PRINT A$;
40 REM (C) FRED BLOGGS 1982
50 GOTO 30
```

Add these extra lines to the program:

```
39 LET A=PEEK 16425+256*PEEK 1
6426
41 POKE A,0
42 POKE A+1,0
43 STOP
```

Now use RUN 39 to make the routine work. Once line 40 has been changed to line 0, delete the extra line. If you like making fools of computers, you can have great fun POKEing all sorts of line numbers into listings. Who said the computer sorts lines into order automatically?

Preventing a screen memory overflow

This routine makes use of the system variable 16442 which refers to the line number of the PRINT position, but does not have the same value as the line number. It starts off at 24 for the top line of the screen, and goes down to 1 for the bottom line. The expression

```
IF PEEK 16442<4 THEN CLS
```

clears the screen automatically if the PRINT position moves to line 21 (the lowest line the user can PRINT on).

Some programs require that the screen be cleared occasionally to prevent a screen memory overflow when the PRINT position gets down to the bottom of the screen. Here is one way to do this:

```
IF PEEK 16442<4 THEN CLS
```

16442 is the system variable containing the line number of the PRINT position. It starts off at 24 for the top line, down to 3 for the lowest line available to the programmer, and 2 and 1 for the two lines at the bottom of the screen used for INPUT, and so on. I have used 4, but you could substitute another number if you like.

Normally you can only PRINT on the top 22 lines of the screen display (lines 0 to 21). Any attempt to use the bottom two lines with PRINT is normally rewarded with an error report 5. You can gain access to these lines by two methods.

The simplest is to POKE directly into memory at the location of the bottom two lines of the screen.

If you have more than 3¼K of memory plugged in (e.g., if you have a 16K RAMPACK) and the display is at full size, line 22 starts at (PEEK 16396 + 256*PEEK 16397 + 727), ends at (PEEK 16396 + 256*PEEK 16397 + 758). Line 23 consequently starts at (PEEK 16396 + 256*PEEK 16397 + 760) and ends at (PEEK 16396 + 256*PEEK 16397 + 791). These addresses will be different if the display file size is altered, as might happen if SCROLL was used. The second method uses PRINT AT and the system variable DF − SZ at address 16418. The number in 16418 says how many lines in the bottom of the screen are not available to the user—normally two. So if we change this number to 0, we have access to all 24 lines of the screen display and we can use PRINT AT 23,X or PRINT AT 22,X.

However, this method comes unstuck when the computer tries to use the bottom of the screen for error reports, IN-PUTS, or even SCROLL. You can get a very nasty systems crash and lose your program if you're unlucky (no lasting damage will be done, but you may have to switch off for a few seconds). The statement POKE 16418,0 must be entered as a line in a program.

It does not work if it is entered as a direct command without a line number, because the computer will reset it automatically when the screen is cleared or a program is RUN. If you wish to use INPUT during the course of a program, then you should POKE 16418,2 to restore the bottom of the screen to normal before attempting to use INPUT, which will of course erase characters PRINTed on line 22 and 23! Incidentally, be careful if you're using an unexpanded machine—the display file behaves in a strange way and makes use of 16418—so try not to upset it too much!

To place any particular line number you require at the top of automatic listings, you must first move the cursor to a line number greater than the one you want at the top (NUMBER is the line you want at the top of the screen). Then enter:

```
POKE 16419,NUMBER-INT (NUMBER/25
6)*256
POKE 16420,INT (NUMBER/256)
```

Now when you press ENTER, the automatic listing will begin where you specified. When entering lines when the cursor is at the bottom of the screen, the computer will usually compile the listing two or three times to get the new line onto the screen listing at the bottom. This is annoying, not to mention time-consuming. You can circumvent this by typing in any line number which does not exist in the listing (we always use 9999) and is *higher* than any shown on screen. The listing will change. If you now continue entering lines where you were originally entering them, they appear near the top of the screen and the listing is made properly, saving a lot of frustration.

CHAPTER 16
Business uses

The computer can be used for a number of small business applications. A wide variety of programs are commercially available to exploit the large potential of the computer. In this section, we'll look at some simple practical application programs for your Sinclair machine.

Money manipulation

James Walsh has written a program to calculate compound interest. The user prompts are clear and easy to follow. The program, as can be seen from the sample input, creates a neat output table.

YEAR	INTEREST	TOTAL
1	$14	$113
2	$15	$127
3	$17	$142
4	$19	$160
5	$21	$180
6	$24	$203
7	$26	$228
8	$30	$257
9	$33	$289
10	$37	$325
11	$42	$365
12	$47	$411
13	$52	$462
14	$59	$520
15	$66	$585
16	$74	$658
17	$83	$741

```
TOTAL= $741
INTEREST= 12.5 PERCENT
ORIGINAL AMOUNT= $100
```

```
50 REM ** COMPOUND INTEREST **
60 REM
70 REM      BY JAMES WALSH
80 REM
90 LET A$=" YEAR    INTEREST
TOTAL"
100 PRINT "NUMBER OF YEARS?"
110 INPUT Y
120 PRINT "AMOUNT?"
130 INPUT A
135 LET T=A
140 PRINT "INTEREST PER ANNUM?"
150 INPUT IN
160 CLS
170 FOR N=1 TO Y
180 SCROLL
190 PRINT AT 0,0;A$
200 GOSUB 340
210 PRINT AT 21,1;N
220 PRINT AT 21,8;"$";INT (V+.5
)
230 PRINT AT 21,19;"$";INT (T+.
5)
240 NEXT N
250 SCROLL
260 SCROLL
270 PRINT "TOTAL= $";INT (T+.5)
280 SCROLL
290 PRINT "INTEREST= ";IN;" PER
CENT"
300 SCROLL
310 PRINT "ORIGINAL AMOUNT= $";
A
320 PRINT AT 0,0;A$
330 STOP
340 LET V=1+(IN/100)*T
350 LET T=(IN/100)*T+T
360 RETURN
```

Let's now look, in a little more detail, at the printing of a column of numbers, a topic which was touched on briefly earlier in the book.

There is something irritating about a list of numbers displayed in a tatty and irregular format. Consider the following versions of the same sum:

99.089	99.09
679.0734	679.07
−2	−2.00
679	679.00

−186	−186.00
46.009	46.01
−269.087	−269.09
−12	−12.00
148	148.00
981.08	981.08
2163.1644	2163.1644

The version on the left was produced by the following routine:

```
100 LET B=0
110 FOR J=1 TO 10
120 INPUT A
130 LET B=B+A
140 PRINT A
160 NEXT J
170 PRINT
190 PRINT B
199 STOP
```

into which, of course, we entered the values which we wanted to add together. This is very untidy.

To start dealing with the problem, modify the program by adding or changing certain lines, as follows:

```
105 LET T=16
140 LET X=A
150 GOSUB 1000
180 LET X=B
190 GOSUB 1000
```

The value of T can be adjusted to change the lateral print position, but be sure to allow sufficient room on the left of the screen for the longest number you want to enter.

The following subroutine, applied to the above, is suitable for any number:

```
1010 LET X$=STR$ X
1020 PRINT TAB T-LEN X$;X$
1029 RETURN
```

If you wish to enter decimal numbers, but only want its nearest integer printed in each case, add the following lines:

```
1000 IF X=.5 THEN LET X=.6
1005 LET X=INT (X+.5)
```

You may want to be able to enter either integer or noninteger values, and to have these printed in full, in which case substitute the following for the whole of subroutine 1000 above.

```
1010 LET X$=STR$ X
1020 IF X$(1)="." THEN LET X$="0
"+X$
1030 FOR K=1 TO LEN X$
1040 IF X$(K)="." THEN GOTO 1070
1050 NEXT K
1060 LET X$=X$+".0"
1080 PRINT TAB T-K;X$
1089 RETURN
```

You may wish to be able to enter negative values, in which case add the following line:

```
1015 IF X<0 THEN IF X$(2)="." TH
EN LET X$=X$(1)+"0"+X$(2 TO )
```

You may wish to print only the first n decimal places. For example, the addition of the following lines would be suitable for cash (i.e., two decimal places):

```
1002 IF X=.005 THEN LET X=.006
1003 IF X=-.005 THEN LET X=-.006
1005 LET X=INT (100*X+.5)/100
1070 IF X$(LEN X$-1)="." THEN LE
T X$=X$+"0"
```

You may wish to put, as we have done in our opening example, the total in complete form, in which case add the following line:

```
1006 IF J=11 THEN LET X=B
```

Another improvement to presentation consists of the addition of the following line:

```
1000 SCROLL
```

You must also amend any PRINT in the main body of the program to SCROLL (e.g., line 170).

Finally, here is a program based on the preceding segments of program which accepts five numbers, adds them together, and—as can be seen from the printout above the listing—prints them out attractively.

Lining up numbers

```
  123.654
     .009
    2.06
   12.60
23333.80

23472.123
```

```
100 LET B=0
105 LET T=16
110 FOR J=1 TO 5
120  INPUT A
130  LET B=B+A
140  LET X=A
150  GOSUB 1000
160 NEXT J
170 PRINT
180 LET X=B
190 GOSUB 1000
199 STOP
1010 LET X$=STR$ X
1020 IF X$(1)="." AND VAL (X$)>.
0999999 THEN LET X$="0"+X$
1030 FOR K=1 TO LEN X$
1040 IF X$(K)="." THEN GOTO 1070
1050 NEXT K
1060 LET X$=X$+"."
1070 IF X$(LEN X$-1)="." OR X$(L
EN X$)="." THEN LET X$=X$+"0"
1080 PRINT TAB T-K;X$
1089 RETURN
```

The material on lining up numbers was prepared by Nick Godwin who also helped write the word processor program that follows. You'll need extra memory to run this program. It will not fit on an unexpanded T/S 1000.

This word processor program will make text neat and tidy before you print it—and gives you the chance to correct mistakes, using a free-moving cursor. You enter your text (up to 17 lines deep) as a single string, X8. When you have the text in, you press ENTER, and the computer will shuffle the words to ensure that none of them are split at the end of a line.

A menu appears with three options: 1—correct the text; 2—LPRINT the text; and 3—start again. If you decide you wish to correct the text, it will reappear on the screen with the words "ENTER 1 TO RETURN TO MENU" above it. You use the 5, 6, 7, and 8 keys to move your cursor in the direction indicated by the arrows on those keys, and the cursor moves along the line of text, inverting the letter it is passing over. Once you find a letter which is wrong, you press A and the words ENTER LETTER TO BE SUB-STITUTED appear at the bottom of the screen. You enter your letter, and press ENTER, and the inverse incorrect letter will be altered to the letter you've chosen. Pressing 1 at any time will return you from the "correction phase" to the original menu, and from this menu you can choose 2 to LPRINT the text.

If you want the text printed, the computer searches through the whole string, turning any inverse letters back to their noninverse equivalents. After LPRINTing, you are shown a further menu, which allows you to run the whole program again from scratch or to terminate the run.

```
20 PRINT "ENTER TEXT"
30 INPUT X$
32 LET X$=X$+"
 "
35 CLS
40 GOSUB 1000
50 PRINT X$
60 PRINT
70 PRINT "ENTER 1 TO CORRECT T
EXT,    2 TO LPRINT, 3 TO ST
ART AGAIN"
80 IF INKEY$="" THEN GOTO 80
100 IF INKEY$="3" THEN RUN
110 IF INKEY$="2" THEN GOTO 400
0
120 IF INKEY$="1" THEN GOTO 200
0
130 GOTO 80
1000 REM STOPS WORD SPLITTING
1010 LET N=1
1020 GOSUB 1180
1030 LET N=N+33
1040 IF N>=LEN X$ THEN RETURN
1045 REM SINGLE SPACE IN
              NEXT LINE
1050 IF X$(N)=" " THEN GOTO 1160
1060 GOSUB 1180
```

```
1065 REM SINGLE SPACE IN
          NEXT LINE
1070 IF X$(N)=" " THEN GOTO 1030
1080 LET J=0
1090 GOSUB 1180
1100 LET J=J+1
1105 REM SINGLE SPACE IN
          NEXT LINE
1110 IF X$(N)>" " THEN GOTO 1090
1120 FOR N=N TO N+J-1
1125 REM SINGLE SPACE IN
          NEXT LINE
1130 LET X$=X$(1 TO N)+" "+X$(N+
1 TO )
1140 NEXT N
1045 REM SINGLE SPACE IN
          NEXT LINE
1050 IF X$(N)=" " THEN GOTO 1160
1060 GOSUB 1180
1065 REM SINGLE SPACE IN
          NEXT LINE
1070 IF X$(N)=" " THEN GOTO 1030
1080 LET J=0
1090 GOSUB 1180
1100 LET J=J+1
1105 REM SINGLE SPACE IN
          NEXT LINE
1110 IF X$(N)>" " THEN GOTO 1090
1120 FOR N=N TO N+J-1
1125 REM SINGLE SPACE IN
          NEXT LINE
1130 LET X$=X$(1 TO N)+" "+X$(N+
1 TO )
1140 NEXT N
1150 GOTO 1030
1160 LET X$=X$(1 TO N-1)+X$(N+
TO )
1170 GOTO 1020
1180 LET N=N-1
1190 RETURN
2000 REM **CORRECTION**
2010 CLS
2020 PRINT "ENTER 1 TO RETURN TO
  MENU"
2030 LET A=1
2035 PRINT AT 2,0;X$
2040 IF INKEY$="" THEN GOTO 2040
2050 IF INKEY$="8" AND A<LEN X$
THEN LET A=A+1
2055 IF INKEY$="6" AND A<LEN X$+
32 THEN LET A=A+32
2060 IF INKEY$="5" AND A>1 THEN
LET A=A-1
```

```
2065 IF INKEY$="7" AND A>32 THEN
  LET A=A-32
2070 IF INKEY$="1" THEN GOTO 70
2075 IF INKEY$="A" THEN GOTO 300
0
2076 PRINT AT 1,0;A;" ";X$(A);"
"
2080 IF CODE X$(A)<128 THEN LET
X$=X$( TO A-1)+CHR$ (CODE X$(A)+
128)+X$(A+1 TO )
2085 IF A=1 THEN GOTO 2035
2090 IF A>1 AND CODE X$(A-1)>127
 THEN LET X$(A-1)=CHR$ (CODE X$(
A-1)-128)
2092 IF A<32 THEN GOTO 2100
2095 IF CODE X$(A-32)>127 THEN L
ET X$(A-32)=CHR$ (CODE X$(A-32)-
128)
2100 IF A<LEN X$-1 AND CODE X$(A
+1)>127 THEN LET X$(A+1)=CHR$ (C
ODE X$(A+1)-128)
2102 IF A<LEN X$-32 THEN GOTO 20
35
2105 IF CODE X$(A+32)>127 THEN L
ET X$(A+32)=CHR$ (CODE X$(A+32)-
128)
2110 GOTO 2035
3000 REM INSERT CORRECTION
3005 PRINT AT 19,0;"INSERT LETTE
R FOR CORRECTION"
3010 INPUT H$
3020 LET X$(A)=H$
3025 PRINT AT 19,0;"
"
3030 GOTO 2035
4000 REM REMOVE INVERSE, LPRINT
4010 FOR G=1 TO LEN X$
4020 IF CODE X$(G)>127 THEN LET
X$(G)=CHR$ (CODE X$(G)-128)
4030 NEXT G
4040 LPRINT X$
4050 CLS
4060 PRINT "ENTER 1 ,TO RUN AGAIN
"
4070 PRINT TAB 5;"2 TO END"
4080 IF INKEY$="" THEN GOTO 4080
4090 IF INKEY$="1" THEN RUN
```

Alphabetizing

The final program in this section is designed to place entries and page references in alphabetical order, and will enable indexes to be constructed (e.g., to books or articles in magazines) or can be easily adapted to accommodate stock lists or levels. You'll need extra memory to run this program. It will not fit on an unexpanded T/S 1000.

The program is based on the string sort given earlier in the book. It is in two parts. The first part (lines 2Ø to 71Ø) accepts the information required, and the second section sorts the data into alphabetical order and then either prints it on the screen or LPRINTs it to the printer.

The program first asks for the title (which is assigned in line 3Ø to T$) and the name of the author (assigned in line 5Ø to A$). The program can cope with 200 entries of up to 32 characters long. The program (see line 685) automatically strips an entry down to 32 characters if one which is too long is entered.

You continue to enter information until you wish to sort and print, when you enter E. The program will then sort the data, and print it item by item.

The format of the output depends, to a large extent, on how you enter the information. Although the program will automatically lay out the title and author fairly well, the format of the entries from this point on depends on how they were entered. The short sample run shows that each entry was made in the form "LAWRENCE − 28," but any other form you desire would be acceptable.

This program has not been set to accommodate the maximum number of entries possible with 16K attached. You can alter parts of the program to trade off length of items against the number of items you want.

If you decided that, for example, 16 characters were long enough for each item, you could make the following changes:

2ØØ   DIM W$(6ØØ,16)
615   Make sure the string is 16 characters long (i.e., that there are 15 spaces after the E)
685   LET W$(A) = W$(A) (TO 16)

This would give you access to 600 items, each up to 16 characters long.

You may wish to modify this program to format the output to your satisfaction.

Sample run:

THROUGH THE WEST
                    HOPPER, C.

```
FRESNO - 43
LOS ANGELES - 51
MEDFORD - 29
MEXICALI - 59
OAKLAND - 56
PASADENA - 47
SALEM - 22
SAN FRANCISCO - 39
SEATTLE - 12
TACOMA - 17
```

The program:

```
   10 REM INDEX
   20 PRINT "ENTER TITLE"
   30 INPUT T$
   40 PRINT "ENTER AUTHOR"
   50 INPUT A$
   60 CLS
  200 DIM W$(200,32)
  300 LET B=0
  400 LET G=0
  500 LET A=1
  600 PRINT AT 2,0;"ENTER SUBJECT
";A;" AND PAGE",""""E""" TO END"
  610 INPUT W$(A)
  615 IF W$(A)="E
               " THEN GOTO 950
  620 PRINT "ITEM ";A;" IS"
  625 PRINT
  630 PRINT W$(A)
  635 PRINT
  640 PRINT "IF THIS IS CORRECT,
PRESS ENTER"
  650 PRINT "IF NOT PRESS ANY KEY
 THEN ENTER"
  660 INPUT Z$
  670 CLS
  680 IF Z$<>"" THEN GOTO 600
  685 LET W$(A)=W$(A)( TO 32)
  690 LET A=A+1
  700 LET G=G+1
  710 GOTO 600
  950 CLS
  960 PRINT "DO YOU WANT A PRINTO
UT (1), OR"
  970 PRINT "JUST ON THE SCREEN (
2)?"
```

```
 975 INPUT Y
 980 SCROLL
 985 IF Y=1 THEN LPRINT T$,,A$
 990 PRINT T$
 991 SCROLL
 992 PRINT ,A$
 993 IF Y=1 THEN LPRINT
 994 SCROLL
 995 LET Z=1
1000 LET B=Z+1
1010 IF B>G THEN GOTO 1090
1020 IF W$(B)>W$(Z) THEN GOTO 10
50
1030 LET Z=Z+1
1040 GOTO 1000
1050 LET O$=W$(Z)
1060 LET W$(Z)=W$(B)
1070 LET W$(B)=O$
1080 GOTO 1030
1090 SCROLL
1100 PRINT W$(G)
1105 IF Y=1 THEN LPRINT W$(G)
1110 LET G=G-1
1120 IF G>0 THEN GOTO 995
```

CHAPTER 17
Improving your programs

You've probably gone through several stages as you have developed your programming skills. After the first, brief struggle with BASIC, you suddenly discovered you could, after a fashion, write programs which ran. They may have looked pretty convoluted when you looked at their listings, and friends may have needed a detailed explanation from you before they knew what to do when running the programs, but at least the programs worked.

There may come a stage when you decide you're going to have to do better than that. But while you may be vaguely dissatisfied with your programs, you may not know how to go about becoming a better programmer. Here are a few guidelines which may help.

First, have a look at a printout of your listing. Programs linked by REM statements look better, and are easier to understand when you return to them after a break. Of course, shortage of memory may preclude the luxury of REM statements, but if you have the memory, you should include them. REM statements filled with just one line of asterisks can prove quite useful in separating each major section of the program. Examine any unconditional GOTO critically. Too many GOTOs leapfrogging over other parts of the program show a lack of directed thinking, make programs run more slowly, and can make them almost impossible to decipher.

It is very good programming practice to have each of the main sections of the program (such as the one which assigns the variables at the beginning of a run, the one which prints out the board, the one which works out who has won, and so on) in separate subroutines. The beginning of your program could well look like this:

```
10 REM *NAME OF PROGRAM*
20 REM ASSIGN VARIABLES
30 GOSUB 9000
40 REM PRINT BOARD
50 GOSUB 8000
60 REM HUMANS MOVE
70 GOSUB 7000
80 REM COMPUTERS MOVE
90 GOSUB 6000
100 REM CHECK IF GAME OVER
110 GOSUB 5000
120 GOTO 50
```

As you can see, this ensures that the program actually cycles through a continuous loop over and over again, until the program terminates within the "CHECK IF GAME OVER" subroutine. You can actually write a series of lines like these before you start writing anything else, and even before you know how you are going to actually perform some of the tasks within the subroutine.

Then you can write the program module by module, making sure that each module works before going on to the next. It is relatively easy to debug a program like this, and far simpler to keep an image of where everything is when you do this than when you just allow a program to, more or less, write itself.

The listing should be, then, as transparent as you can make it, both for your own present debugging, and for future understanding of what part of it carries out what task. The output of the program should also look good. Again, if memory is not a problem, make sure the display is clear and uncluttered. Use blank PRINT lines to space it out, use rules of graphic symbols or whatever to break the screen up into logical sections, and so on. Once you have a program working satisfactorily, it is worth spending extra time on the subroutine which controls the display. Here you'll appreciate again the advantage of having all the display handling in one subroutine, as it will be easy to know where to go to enhance the display.

Of course, as we live in a far from ideal world, it is unlikely that every single display command can be contained within one subroutine, but if you aim toward that end, it will make subsequent working upon the program much easier than it might be otherwise.

The "structured" approach outlined also helps you realize another aim of a good program—to do what you expect it to every time you run it. You should write a program so that, even if you are not present when a friend decides to run it for the first time, it performs as expected. This means not only that it is properly debugged, but that the instructions (which can be contained within the ASSIGN VARIABLES subroutine) are clear and complete.

The user prompts should be clear, so the human operator knows whether to enter a number, a series of numbers, a word, a date, a mixture of letters and numbers, and so on. The program has to assume that the operator is completely ignorant, and that no matter how clearly the instructions and/or user prompts are stated, he or she will attempt to do things the wrong way. A classic example of this is the entering of dates. *Mug traps*, as the routines to reject erroneous input from the operator are called, should be set up to reject a date being entered in a form which the computer cannot understand (such as the day before the month) or which is clearly wrong (such as entering "the 32nd of February"). You should ensure that, no matter what the operator does, the program does not crash or otherwise misbehave. This can happen if the program was expecting a numerical input, and the operator tried to enter a letter or a word. You can get around this by always allowing a string input, going back for another input if the empty string is entered, and taking the VAL or CODE of the input to turn it into numerical form.

Documentation is an area of programming which is often neglected. It is virtually essential for a program which is intended for publication, and most advisable for long programs which you've written for yourself. At the least, the documentation should include a list of variables, an explanation of the program structure (which should be easy to do if you've followed the "modular" approach advised), and brief instructions, especially if the program itself does not contain instructions. A sample run showing the kind of inputs, and the nature and layout of the program outputs, is also useful.

Your program should run as quickly as possible. Every time there is a subroutine or GOTO call, the computer must search through the whole program, line by line, to find the specified line number, so placing often-used subroutines near the beginning of the program will speed them up slightly. That is why the instructions are often placed right at the end. You do not want the computer to have to wade through the initialization and instruction lines every time it has been told to GOTO or GOSUB and is looking for the destination or for the return line number.

Define often-used variables first, so that they will occupy the early slots in the variables store. The computer will search the store only until it finds the variable it wants, so there is no point in getting it to look at more entries than absolutely necessary.

Finally, and this is by far the best way to test a program you've written, call in a friend and sit him or her in front of the TV. Tell your friend to press RUN without you saying anything, and just sit back and watch. If there is any hesitation, or the program "hiccups," you have more work to do.

To summarize:

- Use REM statements.
- Make program listings neat and logical.
- Use structured programming techniques, controlling the program through a loop of subroutine calls.
- Examine unconditional GOTO commands critically.
- Make output displays attractive and clear.
- Ensure that all user prompts are clear.
- Add mug traps on all user input.
- Document your programs, even if you just make a list of variables.
- Make your program run as quickly as possible.
- Test programs by allowing someone unfamiliar with the program to run them.

CHAPTER 18
Converting other BASICs

A wealth of computer programs written in BASIC can be found in a variety of books and computing magazines, but as all versions of BASIC differ to some extent, it is unlikely that a program written to run on another computer will work on your computer without some change. The extent and nature of these changes will depend greatly on the structure of the particular program and how it handles data, but it is possible to give some general guidance on things to look for when approaching the task of converting a "foreign" program to run on your computer.

Multiple statement lines

Some BASICs allow multiple statements on a line, usually separated by : or \, e.g.,

```
10 LET A=B(2)+C:PRINT A,B,C
```

These will have to be written on separate lines for your computer. Beware of multiple statement lines which involve IF/THEN conditional statements. In general, when an IF condition is false, control passes to the next line, not to the next statement. In other words, if the IF condition is false, the entire remainder of the line is skipped over. You should check that the BASIC does in fact operate in this way, and make allowances in your conversion attempts for this.

Integers

The function INT on your machine rounds *down* to the nearest integer. If the program requires that the number be rounded off to the *nearest* integer, then follow this procedure:

If the number to be INTegered is X, then round it off to the nearest integer by using INT(X + 0.5). Note that the PRINT and PLOT commands round off to the nearest integer.

Arrays

The first element of an array on your computer is 1. In some BASICs, there is an additional subscript, 0, which is not available on your machine. Any program which uses the 0 subscript must be altered to start at 1. One quick method (not always guaranteed to work) is to add 1 to each subscript value that you see used in the program. If modifying the subscripts does not work, then the answer is to find out how the program works and rewrite the program so that the correct range of subscripts is obtained.

LEFT$, RIGHT$, MID$

The string operator LEFT$(R$,X) may be replaced by R$(1 TO X) on the computer. This may be shortened to R$(TO X), because 1 is the default value in this case. RIGHT$(R$,X) may be replaced by R$(LEN R$ − X + 1 TO LEN R$), which again may be shortened to R$(LEN R$ − X + 1 TO), because the default value in this case is LEN R$. MID$(R$,J,X) may be replaced by R$(J TO J + X − 1) on the computer.

LET

Some BASICs allow you to omit the LET word when

assigning to a variable, but this is not permitted on the T/S 1000. Therefore, if you come across, say, 200 G = 88, then you must rewrite this as 200 LET G = 88.

GOTO, GOSUB

Some BASICs do not allow a computed GOTO or computed GOSUB, such as GOTO B*30. It may, therefore, be possible to simplify a program using this facility.

ON/GOTO, ON/GOSUB

Often used in some BASICs, these statements are a form of computed GOTO/GOSUB. They make the program GOTO or GOSUB one of a number of lines depending on the value of the variable; for example, 55 ON A GOTO 115,220,333, which will jump to line 115 if I = 1, 220 if I = 2, or 333 if I = 3. The easiest way of converting this statement is by a series of IF/THEN GOTO lines, e.g.,

```
IF A=1 THEN GOTO 115
IF A=2 THEN GOTO 220
IF A=3 THEN GOTO 333
```

However, this is clumsy and wasteful of memory. If the line numbers increment neatly in fixed steps, then it may be possible to use GOTO 500 + 30*A, for example (that is, make use of the computed GOTO/GOSUB facility). Note that although not usually the case, it is sometimes possible to renumber the program to suit.

If the line numbers don't increment in convenient steps, then another possibility is to use "GOTO a conditional expression." For example, ON A GOTO 115,220,333 could be replaced by

```
GOTO (A=1)*115+(A=2)*220+(A=3)*
333
```

Another possibility is

```
GOTO (115 AND A=1)+(220 AND A=2)
+(333 AND A=3)
```

or even

```
GOTO (115 OR A<>1) *(220 OR A<>2)
*(333 OR A<>3)
```

IF/THEN

The expression IF X = 2 THEN 200 is permitted in some BASICs. It means IF X = 2 THEN GOTO 200. You must include the GOTO after THEN on the T/S 1000. Some BASICs insist on having a line number after THEN. The computer can have any command after THEN. You may be able to use this facility to simplify programs on your computer.

FOR/NEXT loops

In many BASICs a FOR/NEXT loop is executed at least once when it is met, even if the end value has already been exceeded, because the test to see if the end value has been exceeded is done at the NEXT statement. On the T/S 1000, if the end value has been exceeded before the loop starts, then the loop is totally and completely bypassed, e.g.,

```
10 FOR A=1 TO 0
20 PRINT A
30 NEXT A
```

will result in nothing being printed, because the computer has realized that 0 is less than the start value, so it skips over the entire loop rather than running through it once. Note that if you added STEP−1, then the computer would perform the loop normally, because it expects the finish value to be less than the start value. In general, this will not present problems unless the control variable is itself set by another variable.

Note also that the variable after NEXT may be omitted on some BASICs, in which case the most recent control variable is incremented. This is not possible on your machine because the control variable must always be specified.

Some BASICs do not like you to jump out of a FOR/NEXT loop before that loop has been finished, and some require the use of a special statement enabling you to jump out of a loop. On the T/S 1000 you can jump out of a loop at will, although the control variable is stored in memory, meaning that you can jump back into that loop if you so desire. However, do not jump into a loop that has not already been executed, since this will cause the program to stop with an error report 1.

END

Sometimes END which stops the program may be omitted altogether, or sometimes it may be replaced by STOP.

PEEK and POKE

There is no easy way to convert statements involving these expressions since their effect will be different on each machine. The only way to convert is to find out what the commands do, then rewrite the statement to perform an equivalent operation on the T/S 1000 if this is possible.

INPUT

You may come across INPUT statements which can accept more than one input value, and perhaps print a prompt string as well. You will have to rewrite this using a PRINT statement for the prompt string, and a separate INPUT for each value required as data. For example, 1Ø input "ENTER YOUR NAME AND AGE"; F8,A.

PRINT

It is highly unlikely that the PRINT format of the computer for which the program was intended will be the same as that of your computer. In certain cases, this will not matter, but if, say, a moving display is required, or a line width exceeds 32 characters, then you may be in trouble. In cases where the spacing across the screen is set up to merely "look pretty," you can easily change this by altering the TAB spacing or adding or omitting spaces in the PRINT statement. Note that programs designed to run on a printer or a screen larger than that of your computer may need changing to prevent a display area overflow. One way of doing this is to have a subroutine to the effect of IF PEEK 16442 < 4 THEN CLS. This works because 16442 stores the line number of the PRINT position on the screen. If the subroutine discovers that the PRINT position has moved the bottom line, or whatever line you insert in the subroutine, then the screen is cleared automatically. Programs written for a printer can often be modified for a SCROLLing display. The only facility on your computer is for an upward SCROLLing display (although a machine-code program can be written for the machine to SCROLL downward or SCROLL only part of the display). Note that the lines in a SCROLLing display on your computer are only as long as they need be—i.e., they are not filled up with spaces as are the normal lines on screens with more than 3¼K of memory attached (according to the system variable RAMTOP)—so you may encounter problems if you attempt to PEEK or POKE the display.

Exponentiation

Some BASICs use the symbols ^ or ← to represent exponentiation; your computer uses shift-H.

DEF, FNR

This is user-defined function, which is mainly a short way of writing an expression. You could replace this by writing the expression out in full each time it is needed, or by adding a subroutine to perform the required calculation. Another method which is not always guaranteed to work is to assign the required calculation to a string variable and use VAL to evaluate the expression, because VAL can evaluate any numeric expressions, including variables and numeric functions. For example, if the original user-defined function reads

```
500 DEF FNR(S)=INT (RND*S)+1
...
2050 LET X=FNR(7)
```

convert it to

```
500 LET A$="INT (RND*S)+1"
...
2040 LET S=7
2050 LET X=VAL A$
```

This performs the same duties as a subroutine can, but you may find it easier to use this method when converting "foreign" BASICs. You will find that in certain applications it can be faster than a subroutine. Note that you can replace the S in line 500 with a number and use this as a routine to generate random numbers, in which case you can omit line 2040. Who knows, subroutines may eventually become redundant!

Random numbers

On machines dealing in real numbers (i.e., machines which are capable of handling floating point numbers), random numbers are usually generated by the expression RND(0) or RND(1) or RND. The number yielded is usually between 0 (which value can be taken) and 1 (which value cannot be taken). This can be directly replaced by RND on your computer. On machines which handle only integer numbers, random numbers are usually generated by the expression RND (X), which usually yields any number from 1 to X inclusive. The equivalent expression on the T/S 1000 is INT (RND*X)+1, which yields an integer in the same range. Since individual BASICs do vary, ensure that the minimum value is 1 and not 0. If so, omit the +1 in your computer's expression. Note that the "random numbers" produced by a computer are not really random, they only appear to be. The computer has a long, long list of stored numbers to use for random numbers. The list is so long you could not possibly spot a pattern in it. Some computers demand a *seed* for the random number, which determines where in the long list of numbers the computer will start.

The RAND function (above the T key) seeds the random number generator with a value related to the number of frames which have been sent to the television since you switched the computer on. This value is not affected by CLEAR or RUN, but is reset to 0 by NEW. You will find that you get numbers which more truly approach random ones by including a line like 1Ø RAND in your programs. However, if you do this, make sure that the program does not go through the line RAND several times during running, as this will produce very "unrandom" numbers indeed. If you use RAND within a program, make sure it is where it will be carried out only once. Alternatively, you can use RAND as a direct command before running a program.

ASC, CODE

ASC returns the ASCII (American Standard Code for Information Interchange) code of the first character in the string. It is similar to your computer's CODE function, except that the numbers yielded are different. There is no easy method to convert values, except if you add 20 to the CODEs of numbers from 0 to 9 and add 27 to your computer's character CODE of any capital letters from A to Z, you will be given the ASCII code of that letter or number. Note that several ASCII characters, including lower-case letters, are not available on your machine.

READ, DATA, RESTORE

Most BASICs allow you to write a list of data elements in the program. When the program is RUN, a READ statement is then used to transfer the values to an array. The simplest way of converting is to replace the lot with a list of LET statements. This can be very tedious and consume a lot of memory if there are several values. A better method is to use the routine in the section Printing String Arrays that is presented earlier in this book. First declare an array with sufficient dimensions and enter the elements individually by means of a loop. Then delete the initialization program, and save the rest of the program on tape using the load and go routine, to avoid any risk of starting the program with RUN and deleting all your carefully preserved variables.

Another method is to set up a string array long enough to accommodate all the data in one string, and to then set up a numeric array so that the first element says where the first word or data element starts, the second says where it ends, the third indicates the start of the second word or data element, the fourth the end of that second data element, and so on. Here's an example of this in use. The computer will achieve the amazingly difficult task of telling you which month your birthday falls in if you give it the number of that month.

You will need two arrays, A$ and B$. A$ holds information concerning the location of words in B$. B$ may be up to 999 characters in length with three-digit storage in A$. You will need to alter several things in the program to change the number of digits that store information in A$. You also need a numeric variable A, which tells the computer which word you want to extract from the data string B$. If you like, A can be the number of the word you READ from the DATA string. There is no need for a RESTORE command, since variable A can simply be reset to 1 if you wanted to READ words from B$ in turn. You should include a line to preclude unwanted values of A (in this case, less than 1 or greater than 12) since these will constitute a subscript error and cause the program to STOP with error report 3. Here is the routine:

```
10 LET A$="001008016021026029
030037043052059067075"
20 LET B$="JANUARYFEBRUARYMARC
HAPRILMAYJUNEJULYAUGUSTSEPTEMBER
OCTOBERNOVEMBERDECEMBER"
30 PRINT "ENTER THE NUMBER OF
THE MONTH YOU WERE BORN IN?"
40 INPUT A
50 IF A<1 OR A>12 THEN GOTO 40
60 LET A=(A-1)*3
70 PRINT "SO YOU WERE BORN IN
";B$(VAL A$(A+1 TO A+3) TO VAL A
$(A+4 TO A+6)-1)
```

The numbers in string A$ are arranged in groups of three to simplify decoding. For instance, the first three digits refer to the starting position of the first word (001), the second set of three digits to the starting position of the second word (008) and so on. You may have noticed that there are three extra digits at the end of A$ that refer to a nonexistent element—in fact, it is one greater than the position of the last character in B$ and is necessary for the correct functioning of the routine. This is because, to find the end of a word, the routine looks for the beginning of the next word and subtracts one from its starting position. As it stands, the routine allows you to store up to 999 characters of DATA because the starting positions are stored as three digits, giving you a maximum number of 999. To store more DATA than this, you need to store the information in A$ in four digits and change the decoding as necessary in lines 60 and 70. Remember that the maximum value of A allowed in line 50 should be the same as the number of words in B$. It may be less if you want to restrict the amount of words available, e.g., anybody with a birthday later than OCTOBER was not allowed to use the program!

The routine runs fairly quickly, and if you want to test its speed, make the following changes to the routine. Try deleting line 30:

```
40 LET A=INT (RND*12)+1
70 PRINT B$(VAL A$(A+1 TO A+3)
TO VAL A$(A+4 TO A+6)-1);" ";
80 GOTO 40
```

Integer arithmetic

In general, always add the function INT before a division in a program designed for a computer with integer arithmetic. You may require parentheses around the division so that INT works only on the result of that division.

Logical expressions

Most BASICs allow expressions to be evaluated as true or false. On your computer, a true expression returns a value of 1, a false returns a value of 0. Some BASICs return −1 for a true expression. The particular method of conversion used will depend on the context in which the expression is used. It may be possible to negate the result by simply adding the − symbol to the expression, e.g., LET A = B = C may be replaced by LET A = −(B = C). This method will not work all the time, and hence it may be necessary to completely rewrite the expression for it to work properly on your computer.

DIM

Some BASICs allow you to write several DIM statements on one line, e.g., DIM A8(9), B8(8), C8(7). You will have to replace this by individual DIM statements on separate program lines. If the program calls for arrays with names that are more than one letter long, then these have to be replaced by single-letter names like A8 or B. If you do not have enough letters available, then you may be able to declare additional dimensions to the existing ones for a certain array and use the extra dimension to replace an array. Programs that cause this problem are generally too long to fit into a standard T/S machine anyhow. Beware of the zero subscripts!

GET, GET8

This is a function that reads characters or values from keys pressed on the keyboard. It takes various forms on various computers, but in general it waits until a key is pressed before it goes on, assigning either the character corresponding to the key pressed or the code of that character to a variable, for example, GET A8 or LET A8 = GET8. You could do this on your computer:

```
1000 LET A$=INKEY$
1010 IF A$="" THEN GOTO 1000
```

This would return the character corresponding to the key pressed on the keyboard. If the function was to return the CODE of the character (note that this would be ASCII code, which returns completely different values to the T/S CODE values), then use this routine:

```
1000 LET A$=INKEY$
1010 IF A$="" THEN GOTO 1000
1020 LET A=CODE A$
```

The version that returns a numeric value rather than a character code is slightly different. It is necessary to ensure that the character read from the keyboard is in the range from 0 to 9 so that we can apply VAL to convert the character to a number. Here's one way:

```
1000 LET A$=INKEY$
1010 IF A$<"0" OR A$>"9" THEN GO
TO 1000
1020 LET A=VAL A$
```

You may also come across a version of INKEY$ which allows a time limit to be specified for a user response, e.g.,

```
100 LET A$=INKEY$ (X)
```

where X specifies the time limit. This can be converted in two ways:
First,

```
100 PAUSE X
110 LET A$=INKEY$
```

and second,

```
100 FOR A=0 TO X
110 LET A$=INKEY$
120 IF A$<>"" THEN GOTO 131
130 NEXT A
```

You will need to change the value of X for both routines to give the required time delay.

VAL

If the argument of VAL does not form a valid numerical argument, you get an error report. Other BASICs return 0.

SET, RESET

These are used to make a particular screen point white or black. Replace with a PLOT/UNPLOT/PRINT AT.

Drawing diagonal lines on screen

Some BASICs have a function that draws a line between two given sets of coordinates. The straightness and smoothness of this line is determined by the resolution with which the machine used can PLOT or PRINT the line. As your computer does not sport high-resolution graphics, and PLOTs on a 64-by-44 matrix, the lines produced are not impressive compared with more expensive high-resolution machines. This small routine allows you to draw lines through two given sets of points. It may use PLOT or PRINT AT, and instructions are given to enable you to use either. You enter the coordinates in the following order:

1.   X coordinate you wish to start drawing *from*
2.   Y coordinate you wish to start drawing *from*
3.   X coordinate you wish to draw *to*
4.   Y coordinate you wish to draw *to*

For instance, if you entered

Ø ENTER
Ø ENTER
63 ENTER
43 ENTER

you would see a line being PLOTted from the bottom left side of the screen up toward the top right side of the screen. It is quite fast to execute: The longest time to PLOT any line is 7 seconds and the longest time to PRINT any line is 4 seconds. This applies to lines drawn across the full width of the screen. Shorter lines take correspondingly less time. You can use this routine to PLOT or PRINT one pixel or character if you want, simply by entering the same pair of coordinates twice when prompted. This routine takes less than 300 bytes for the program and variables, and extra for the screen:

```
8010 INPUT X
8020 INPUT Y
8030 INPUT X1
8040 INPUT Y1
8050 LET A=X-X1
8060 LET B=Y-Y1
```

```
8070 LET C=(A AND ABS A)=ABS B) +
(B AND ABS B>ABS A)
8080 IF C=0 THEN LET C=0.1
8090 FOR F=0 TO C STEP SGN C
8100 PLOT X+A/C*-F,Y+B/C*-F
8110 NEXT F
```

To PRINT AT rather than PLOT the line, change line 8100 like this:

```
9000 PRINT AT Y+B/C*-F,X+A/C*-F;
"■"
```

The INPUTs are not idiot-proofed at the moment; that is, you can enter values which cause the program to crash or produce undesirable results. You may want to modify the program yourself to protect it against you and others. You can use one of two methods to do this. You can check each INPUT after it has been entered with a line like IF X<0 OR X>63 THEN GOTO 8010. Alternatively, you can modify the loop to PRINT or PLOT only pixels or characters if their locations are actually on screen and ignore those coordinates that are off screen.

Remember that this is a subroutine rather than a program in itself, although you can use it as a program if you add a line:

```
8120 GOTO 8010
```

This will allow you to draw all sorts of lines to demonstrate the routine. Try drawing a frame around the screen and lines from corner to corner. Experiment with the PRINT AT and PLOT versions and see what they can both do. If you want anything other than black lines (e.g., letters), then you'll obviously have to use PRINT AT.

ELSE

This is an extension to the IF/THEN conditional statement and allows more than one outcome depending on whether the conditional statement is true or false. It may be replaced by two conditional expressions on your computer. For example,

```
20 IF X=1 THEN LET Y=7 ELSE GOTO
80
```

may be replaced by

```
20 IF X=1 THEN LET Y=7
21 IF X<>1 THEN GOTO 80
```

If the action of ELSE is to assign one of several alternative values to a variable, then it can be replaced on one line; e.g.,

```
50 IF X=1 THEN LET Y=7 ELSE LET
Y=8
```

may be replaced by

```
 50 LET Y=(7 AND X=1)+(8 AND X<
>1)
```

Certain expressions such as the one above may be replaced by even shorter forms:

```
50 LET Y=7+(1 AND X<>1)
```

No general guideline can be given since the method used will vary from example to example. However, the examples above should give you an idea of what to expect.

You may come across a statement where the action performed by ELSE is itself conditional:

```
10 IF X=1 THEN LET Y=1 ELSE IF X
=5 THEN GOTO 100
```

This will need to be rewritten as either

```
 10 IF X=1 THEN LET Y=1
 11 IF X<>1 THEN IF X=5 THEN GO
TO 100
```

or

```
 10 IF X=1 THEN LET Y=1
 11 IF X<>1 AND X=5 THEN GOTO 1
00
```

Again, you may meet all sorts of conditional ELSEs, and the T/S version will depend on the variation encountered.

REPEAT/UNTIL

This is a loop that performs an operation continuously, ending only when a specified condition is met. Its use is so wide that it is difficult to specify a universal method of conversion to T/S BASIC, probably the best being the IF/THEN GOTO conditional statement. Here is an example:

```
10 PRINT "ENTER YES OR NO"
20 REPEAT
30 INPUT A$
40 UNTIL A$="YES" OR A$="NO"
```

may be replaced by:

```
10 PRINT "ENTER YES OR NO"
20 INPUT A$
30 IF A$<>"YES" AND A$<>"NO" THEN GOTO 20
```

REPEAT/UNTIL structures are generally far more complex than this example, and it may be necessary to find a means of conversion other than IF/THEN GOTO. For example, where the value of a variable is the determining factor, a FOR/NEXT loop may sometimes be used. However, the possibility of using an IF/THEN GOTO conditional statement should always be considered and is sometimes the only successful method of conversion.

Undefined variables

If you attempt to use a variable before it has been defined or assigned to in a program, some computers will return a value of 0. You get error report 2 on your computer if the variable has not previously been assigned to. When using programs on your computer which use variables, these variables must all be assigned to.

Matrices

Some BASICs have matrix functions which perform operations on arrays. Your computer does not have these functions, so you will have to perform the operations on array elements individually, possibly by means of a loop.

```
10 DIM X(Y)
20 DIM P(Y)
30 MAT X=P
```

This particular example can be replaced by

```
10 LET N=0
20 DIM X(Y)
30 DIM P(Y)
40 LET N=N+1
50 IF N<Y THEN GOTO 40
```

PROC, ENDPROC

This is a method of using subroutines to do certain procedures in such a way that among other things makes programs and listings easier to understand and read (this is called *structured programming* by some). It enables subroutines to be used specifically to do certain things, and it is like a subroutine in many ways, but with the important exception that it is called by a name rather than by its line numbers. Take this example, which prints the score on the screen:

```
100 PROCSCORE
...
1000 DEF PROCSCORE
1010 PRINT "SCORE=";S
1020 ENDPROC
```

ENDPROC is similar to RETURN in that the procedure comes to an end and the program resumes from the line after the one which called the procedure, in this case the line after line 100. The name of the procedure is not used in your computer's version, although it can be adapted for the purpose as the second example of the Sinclair version will show. The simplest method of conversion to T/S BASIC is for line 100 to GOSUB line 1000, possibly have a REM statement somewhere in the subroutine to identify it, and end the subroutine with a RETURN command.

```
100 GOSUB 1000
.....
1000 REM SCORE SUBROUTINE
1010 PRINT "SCORE=";S
1020 RETURN
```

If you want to retain the procedure/subroutine naming facility, you can use a variable of the same name as the PROC name assigned during the course of the program before the subroutine is called, and use this variable as the destination for the GOSUB command. You could include a REM statement in the subroutine to identify the subroutine and tie it up with the variable name used. It is useful to use inverse characters in these REM statements so that they stand out from the rest of the listing text. Therefore, you can make your programs seem fairly structured if you like.

```
   50 LET SCORE=1000
......
  100 GOSUB SCORE
......
 1000 REM SCORE SUBROUTINE
 1010 PRINT "SCORE=";S
 1020 RETURN
```

Although PROCs may be complex, an ordinary subroutine is the best method of conversion to your BASIC using GOSUB/RETURN.

INSTR(A$,B$)

There is a function that looks to see if there is a copy of B$ in A$, and if there is, it tells you where the copy starts. For instance, if B$ was "PUT" and A$ was "COMPUTER," then the value of INSTR(A$,B$) would be 4 because the part of A$ which held the letters "PUT" started at the fourth element of A$. If the function does not find a copy of B$ in A$, then INSTR(A$,B$) has a value of 0. A special routine has to be written to provide this function on your computer.

Here is one method of converting this function to run on the T/S.

```
1000 REM --LET X=INSTR(A$,B$)--
1010 LET Y=0
1020 IF LEN A$=0 OR LEN B$=0 OR
LEN B$>LEN A$ THEN RETURN
1030 FOR Y=1 TO LEN A$-LEN B$+1
1040 IF A$(Y TO Y+LEN B$-1)=B$ T
HEN RETURN
1050 NEXT Y
1060 LET Y=0
1070 RETURN
```

Note that if you want to detect whole words rather than just strings, you will have to examine A$ for spaces or punctuation marks that signify the start and end of words. The routine above just finds matching strings, so that if you wanted to find the word CAT in a phrase containing the word CATA-STROPHIC, this would trigger on the first three letters of CATASTROPHIC. Users of INSTR usually have this problem, so the program will cater for this anyway!

DIV

DIV gives the whole-number part of the result of a division, for example, 17 DIV 5 gives 3. INT can be applied to the result of the division on your computer. So A DIV B on the T/S 1000 would be INT (A/B).

MOD

MOD gives the *remainder* of a division, e.g., 17 MOD 5 is 2. A MOD B is A − (INT (A/B)*B) on the computer. Note that TAB carries out its own MOD action (modulo 32) on your computer.

Cursor movement

Certain programs may require the use of cursor control codes to backspace over text or move the PRINT position. Where the cursor movement is absolute, a simple PRINT AT Y,X; may suffice. Screen formats vary greatly, and since your computer has one of the lowest resolution screens around (32 by 22 characters), displays may prohibit the use of the same cursor controls. Where cursor movement is relative (e.g., backspace 1 character), the following may help: Use the values contained in the system variables 16441 (PRINT column number) and 16442 (PRINT line number) to control the PRINT position. The values contained in these system variables do not correspond to the normal PRINT AT Y,X; values. The PRINT line number (16442) starts off at 24 for a Y coordinate of Ø. The PRINT column number (16441) starts off at 33 for an X coordinate of Ø. So to move the PRINT cursor (!) up one position we could use:

```
PRINT AT 24-PEEK 16442-1,33-PEEK
  16441;
```

To move the PRINT position down one line we could use:

```
PRINT AT 24-PEEK 16442+1,33-PEEK
  16441;
```

To move the PRINT position one position to the right:

```
PRINT AT 24-PEEK 16442,33-PEEK 1
6441+1;
```

And to move the PRINT position one position to the left (provided the last PRINT statement ended with a semicolon this could be used to erase the last character printed!):

```
PRINT AT 24-PEEK 16442,33-PEEK 1
6441-1;
```

You could save all this trouble if you used a variable to control the PRINT position as you would in a moving-graphics program.

' (apostrophe)

The ' symbol is used on some computers to move the PRINT position down one line. Where it is used to move the PRINT position to the start of the next line, a simple PRINT TAB Ø; will suffice on your computer. Where it is used to move the PRINT position to the same point on the line below, you could use the techniques described in the previous paragraph on cursor movement.

SCREENS, POINT

These functions return information as to the state of the screen at a specified location. The best way of conversion is to move the PRINT position to this location by PRINT AT Y,X; and then use the system variable DF-CC in addresses

16398/16399 to tell you where the PRINT position is located in the display file, and then PEEK this address. It sounds complicated, but this is all you do:

```
LET P=PEEK (PEEK 16398+256*PEEK
16399)
```

The variable P now contains the CODE of the character at screen coordinates Y,X. If you wish to return the actual character rather than its CODE, merely add:

```
LET P$=CHR$ (P)
```

TAB

Some computers may have two arguments to the TAB function, which is used to space out along the screen. This use of TAB conforms to your computer's use of AT. For example, TAB (X,Y) on some computers would correspond to AT Y,X; on your machine. The X and Y coordinates may be in reverse order on some computers.

Degrees and radians

Your T/S 1000 deals with trigonometric functions in radians. Degrees may be converted to radians by this expression:

```
LET RADIANS=(PI*DEGREES) /180
```

and radians may be converted to degrees by:

```
LET DEGREES=(PI*RADIANS) /180
```

Base-10 logarithms

As your computer works in natural logarithms, to base e, if you need logs base 10 for any reason, these may be found using the expression

```
LET LOGBASE10 (X)=(LN (X) /(LN(10
))
```

You could use this to find logs for any base. Suppose you wanted the log base b of X:

```
LET LOGBASEB (X)=(LN (X)/(LN(B))
```

Happy calculations!

% (percent symbol)

The percent symbol is generally used to specify an integer variable, e.g., A%. Integer variables are usually used to save memory or because they can be processed more quickly than conventional variables. In general, there is no harm in using an ordinary variable, although you should be wary of these integer variables being assigned as the result of a division— they automatically truncate the quotient to its integer value. In such a case use LET A = INT (A/2), for example, to "integerize" the result of the division.

? (question mark)

On most computers the symbol ? is used as an abbreviation for the PRINT command.

APPENDIX

Byte watching

What does this mean?

If you only have a 2K RAM computer, you will find yourself rather short of space to write programs in. It is necessary, therefore, to make sure that programs are written with as little wastage of space as is possible. Sometimes it is a case of *how* something is written rather than how much space is wasted. This section deals with some methods of saving space; you will find other methods as you continue to program.

Just how much space have I got?

The system variables (that tell the computer little things about itself) occupy a fixed amount of memory from 16384 to 16508, so that's 125 bytes lost straight away, although three of them are not used. If there's nothing printed on the screen, then the display file occupies just 25 bytes (containing 25 NEWLINE characters or CHR$ 118's) and this grows as and when you PRINT anything on the screen; e.g., if you PRINT "HELP", the display file grows by four bytes. So if you fill the screen, you have 22 lines of 32 characters each plus the 25 NEWLINE characters, making 726 bytes in all. An empty screen means that there are 874 bytes available for program, display, variables, work space, and the various stacks. A full screen on the other hand leaves only 173 or the first 1024 bytes.

Why do programs need more space than on the ZX80, the T/S 1000's predecessor?

There are several reasons. First, line numbers are followed in a listing by two invisible bytes storing the length of the line. This was not used on the ZX80. Numbers need six extra bytes, which you don't see in the listing, because the number is stored twice—in a form as typed into the T/S 1000 and also in a five-byte format following a CHR$ 126 (telling the computer that this is a number, so don't print it in a listing), which is a form which enables the computer to handle the number more easily and quickly. None of the six bytes were used on the ZX80. So a single-digit number needs seven bytes to store in a program on your computer, compared with only two bytes on the ZX80. Also, numeric arrays need five bytes for every element, compared with only two on the ZX80, plus a byte to say how many dimensions you've given to the array (even if it's only one). Then there are extra bytes for every dimension you give the array. This also applies to string arrays. FOR/NEXT loops use extra bytes as well—the initial value is stored in five bytes as is the limit value (as opposed to two each on the ZX80). There are an additional five bytes that specify the value of STEP, even if it is not specified in the listing.

How do I go about saving space?

1. Numbers are the most obvious target. If you don't mind slowing the program down slightly, you can store the number in a string and decode it using VAL or CODE. CODE is slightly faster than VAL, so if your numbers range from 0 to 255, you can put the character whose code is that number in quotes and save a few bytes every time; e.g., 2Ø LET A = 2 takes three more bytes than 2Ø LET A = VAL "2" or 2Ø LET A = CODE "▓". If your number is more than one digit long, you may find that your program listing becomes a bit hard to follow as a result, particularly if you use one of the characters PRINTed as ?. For example, 5Ø or 128, and then 2Ø

LET A = CODE "M" and 2Ø LET A = CODE "█" save one and two bytes respectively over 2Ø LET A = VAL "5Ø" and 2Ø LET A = VAL "128". If you use a particular number at least four times in a program, it may be worth storing that number as a variable and using the variable instead of the number throughout the program.

2. Line numbers are another target. If you have several consecutive PRINT or IF/THEN statements, it may be possible to combine these as a single line, saving line numbers and line length markers. You can have any combination of PRINT/TAB/AT on a single program line, all linked by semicolons, so you can replace

```
10 PRINT TAB 12; "THE"
20 PRINT AT 2,12; "FORCE"
30 PRINT AT 4,12; "RULES"
```

with 1Ø PRINT TAB 12; "THE"; AT 2,12; "FORCE"; AT 4,12; "RULES" saving 10 bytes in all (4 for the two line numbers, 4 for the two line length markers, and 2 NEWLINE characters).

Conditional statements can often be reduced to one line from several, using either the logical operators AND and OR or the true/false values of 1 and 0; for instance,

```
10 IF INKEY$="8" THEN LET X=X+1
20 IF INKEY$="5" THEN LET X=X-1
```

may be rewritten as

```
10 LET X=X-(INKEY$="5")+(INKEY
$="8")
```

saving a mighty 23 bytes!

You can apply this to conditional PRINTs as well:

```
10 IF X=1 THEN PRINT "ONE"
20 IF X=2 THEN PRINT "TWO"
```

takes three more bytes than

```
10 PRINT ("ONE" AND X=1)+("TWO"
AND X=2)
```

This comes into its own if you have several alternatives which can be combined on one line. You can extend this to GOTO and GOSUB as well:

```
10 IF X=1 THEN GOTO 500

20 IF X=2 THEN GOTO 660

30 IF X=3 THEN GOTO 777
```

occupies seven more bytes than

```
10 GOTO (X=1) *500+(X=2) *660+
(X=3) *777
```

You will have noticed that these all involve replacing a series of IF/THEN statements with several conditional expressions on one line. You may discover several other ways of using this facility, and they usually all save small amounts of memory.

3. PRINTing on screen uses up varying amounts of memory if you have less than 3¼K of memory in use, because your computer fills up a line on the screen with spaces up to where you've started PRINTing. So PRINTing on the right-hand side of the screen will use up more memory than PRINTing on the left-hand side. Try to PRINT on the left side of the screen if you're short of memory. Frequent use of CLS to clear up redundant material on screen can help greatly.

4. If you want to store information, you can place it in some of the system variables that are POKEable. (For example, you can use the unused threesome of 16417, 16507, and 16508 and the printer buffer from 16444 to 16476 if the printer is not being used at the time. Like all system variables from 16393 onwards, the values stored in these are saved on tape.)

5. When you type a line like 50 LET Y=5, then when the program is RUN, the variable Y is copied into the variables area and occupies 6 bytes there as well as 15 in the program area. If you are short of memory, you can enter LET Y=5 as a direct command, leave out line 50, and start the program with a GOTO command, and you have saved 15 bytes every time. Beware though—if you

    enter RUN or CLEAR, then you've lost your variables, so only use this as a last resort.

6. If you want to generate random numbers several times in a program, then you could either do this in a subroutine, or have a string variable like LET A$ = INT (RND*10) + 1''. Every time you want a random number you can type LET A = VAL A$, which surprisingly enough works because VAL sees the expression in A$ as being a valid numerical expression.

7. Finally, the golden rule. If you can't make a program fit into the amount of memory on your computer, try rewriting the program completely to see if you can find a shorter way of doing the same thing.

How can I find out how much memory I've used up?

There are several methods depending on what you want to know. If you want to find or compare the length of just the listing, all you need to do is find where the display file starts, since this always follows on from where the program ends. Use this expression as a direct command, since it is dealt with by an area of memory independent of the program and therefore does not affect the result:

```
PRINT PEEK 16396+256*PEEK 16397
```

This gives you the start of the display file. To obtain the length of the program, we need to subtract the address of where the program starts, which is always 16509. So we can rewrite the expression as:

```
PRINT PEEK 16396+256*PEEK
16397- 16509
```

If you substituted 16384 for the 16509 in the expression above, then you would get an answer that included the system variables as well as the program.

A very useful expression is PRINT PEEK 16404 + 256*PEEK 16405-16384, which tells you the number of bytes you've used for system variables, program, variables, and display. Used in a program, it gives a figure that includes space currently used by the display, variables, system variables, and program. If you want to use it just once or twice that's fine, but if you're likely to use it very often, you may like to use this machine code routine. Use a hex loader to enter these bytes of hex into spare memory above RAMTOP or in a REM statement at the beginning of the program. You will need 13 bytes for the routine.

HEX	ASSEMBLER	NOTES
2A1440	LD HL, (16404)	Copy the E-line system variable into the HL register pair.
010040	LD BC, 16384	Load address of start of RAM into the BC register pair.
C600	ADD A,0	Reset carry flag to 0.
ED42	SBC HL, BC	Subtract BC from HL.
44	LD B,H	Copy H register contents into B register.
4D	LD C,L	Copy L register contents into C register.
C9	RET	Return to BASIC.

If you PRINT USR 30000 (or whatever the start address of the routine is), you will quickly get your value. Provided you don't switch off and the routine is placed in RAM above the address in RAMTOP, you can happily LOAD and RUN programs without affecting the routine, so it is always there when needed.

```
HEX                      ASSEMBLER
---                      ---------

2A1440                   LD  HL, (16404)
010040                   LD  BC, 16384
C600                     ADD A, 0
ED42                     SBC HL, BC
44                       LD  B, H
4D                       LD  C, L
C9                       RET
```

Code Character Tables

CODE	CHARACTER	CODE	CHARACTER	CODE	CHARACTER
Ø	space	28	Ø	56	S
1	▫	29	1	57	T
2	◰	30	2	58	U
3	▰	31	3	59	V
4	▝	32	4	6Ø	W
5	▰	33	5	61	X
6	▰	34	6	62	Y
7	▰	35	7	63	Z
8	▰	36	8	64	RND
9	▰	37	9	65	INKEY$
1Ø	▰	38	A	66	PI
11	"	39	B	67	not used
12	£	40	C	68	not used
13	$	41	D	69	not used
14	:	42	E	7Ø	not used
15	?	43	F	71	not used
16	(	44	G	72	not used
17	)	45	H	73	not used
18	>	46	I	74	not used
19	<	47	J	75	not used
2Ø	=	48	K	76	not used
21	+	49	L	77	not used
22	−	5Ø	M	78	not used
23	×	51	N	79	not used
24	/	52	O	8Ø	not used
25	;	53	P	81	not used
26	,	54	Q	82	not used
27	.	55	R	83	not used

CODE	CHARACTER	CODE	CHARACTER	CODE	CHARACTER
84	not used	111	not used	138	■
85	not used	112	cursor up	139	"
86	not used	113	cursor down	140	£
87	not used	114	cursor left	141	$
88	not used	115	cursor right	142	:
89	not used	116	GRAPHICS	143	?
90	not used	117	EDIT	144	(
91	not used	118	ENTER	145	)
92	not used	119	RUBOUT	146	>
93	not used	120	K or L mode	147	<
94	not used	121	FUNCTION	148	=
95	not used	122	not used	149	+
96	not used	123	not used	150	−
97	not used	124	not used	151	×
98	not used	125	not used	152	/
99	not used	126	number	153	;
100	not used	127	cursor	154	,
101	not used	128	■	155	.
102	not used	129	◱	156	0
103	not used	130	◳	157	1
104	not used	131	▬	158	2
105	not used	132	◲	159	3
106	not used	133	◰	160	4
107	not used	134	◪	161	5
108	not used	135	◩	162	6
109	not used	136	▓	163	7
110	not used	137	▞	164	8

CODE	CHARACTER	CODE	CHARACTER	CODE	CHARACTER
165	9	192	" "	219	< =
166	A	193	AT	220	> =
167	B	194	TAB	221	< >
168	C	195	not used	222	THEN
169	D	196	CODE	223	TO
170	E	197	VAL	224	STEP
171	F	198	LEN	225	LPRINT
172	G	199	SIN	226	LLIST
173	H	200	COS	227	STOP
174	I	201	TAN	228	SLOW
175	J	202	ASN	229	FAST
176	K	203	ACS	230	NEW
177	L	204	ATN	231	SCROLL
178	M	205	LN	232	CONT
179	N	206	EXP	233	DIM
180	O	207	INT	234	REM
181	P	208	SQR	235	FOR
182	Q	209	SGN	236	GOTO
183	R	210	ABS	237	GOSUB
184	S	211	PEEK	238	INPUT
185	T	212	USR	239	LOAD
186	U	213	STR$	240	LIST
187	V	214	CHR$	241	LET
188	W	215	NOT	242	PAUSE
189	X	216	**	243	NEXT
190	Y	217	OR	244	POKE
191	Z	218	AND	245	PRINT

CODE	CHARACTER
246	PLOT
247	RUN
248	SAVE
249	RAND
250	IF
251	CLS
252	UNPLOT
253	CLEAR
254	RETURN
255	COPY

Error report codes

Ø   Successful completion of program or direct command.

1   NEXT with no FOR, but there is a variable of the same name.

2   This means an undefined variable has been used. It can be an undefined string (A$), numerical variable (like A or ZP4), or an element of a string or numeric array (such as A$(4) when DIM A$(4) has not been used previously in the program). The error also comes up if the computer comes across a NEXT line, where there is no FOR of that name, and the *control letter* of the loop (like A in FOR A = 1 TO 50) has not previously been used as a variable in the program.

3   Subscript out of range. This will occur when, for example, the array has been set up to cope with four elements— DIM A(4)—and reference was made to A(5). If the subscript is negative or greater than 65535, the error code B will be given.

4   Memory is full.

5   Screen is full.

6   Arithmetic overflow.

7   RETURN with no corresponding GOSUB.

8   INPUT used as a command.

9   Program halted by STOP.

A   Invalid argument to certain functions.

B   Integer out of range.

C   The text of the (string) argument of VAL does not form a valid numerical expression.

D   Program stopped by BREAK or by a STOP command entered in an INPUT statement.

E   Not used.

F   No program name given for SAVE.

Keyboard layout

WORD	HOW OBTAINED	WORD	HOW OBTAINED
ABS	FUNCTION G	LN	FUNCTION Z
AND	SHIFT 2	LOAD	J
ARCCOS	FUNCTION S	LPRINT	SHIFT S
ARCSIN	FUNCTION A	NEW	A
ARCTAN	FUNCTION D	NEXT	N
AT	FUNCTION C	NOT	FUNCTION N
BREAK	SPACE	OR	SHIFT W
CHRS	FUNCTION U	PAUSE	M
CLEAR	X	PEEK	FUNCTION O
CLS	V	PI/π	FUNCTION M
CODE	FUNCTION I	PLOT	Q
CONT	C	POKE	O
COPY	Z	PRINT	P
COS	FUNCTION W	RAND	T
CURSOR ⟺	SHIFT 5	REM	E
CURSOR ⟺	SHIFT 6	RETURN	Y
CURSOR ⟺	SHIFT 7	RND	FUNCTION T
CURSOR ⟺	SHIFT 8	RUBOUT	SHIFT Ø
DIM	D	RUN	R
EDIT	SHIFT 1	SAVE	S
EXP	FUNCTION X	SCROLL	B
FAST	SHIFT F	SGN	FUNCTION F
FOR	F	SIN	FUNCTION Q
FUNCTION	SHIFT ENTER	SLOW	SHIFT D
GOSUB	H	SQR	FUNCTION H
GOTO	G	STEP	SHIFT E
GRAPHICS	SHIFT 9	STOP	SHIFT A
IF	U	STRS	FUNCTION Y
INKEYS	FUNCTION B	TAB	FUNCTION P
INPUT	I	TAN	FUNCTION E
INT	FUNCTION R	THEN	SHIFT 3
LEN	FUNCTION K	TO	SHIFT 4
LET	L	UNPLOT	W
LIST	K	USR	FUNCTION L
LLIST	SHIFT G	VAL	FUNCTION J

Punctuation marks, arithmetic signs, graphics symbols, numbers, and letters are not shown in this table. They can be found more quickly on the keyboard than in a chart like the one on page 193, because there is no simple and obvious method of listing them like the alphabetic characters on page 193.

The symbols on the left-hand side of the chart on page 195 are the first hex digits, the symbols along the top are the second hex digits. This table should only be used for numbers from 0 to 255 decimal.

To convert numbers to hex in the range 0 to 65535, follow this procedure. Suppose the number is X. The first two hex digits may be found by converting the value obtained by INT(X/256) using the table on page 195. Then, the remaining two digits are obtained by converting the value obtained from X-(INT(X/256))*256 using the table on page 195.

decimal loader

```
 1 REM 123456789
10 LET A=15514
20 INPUT B
30 SCROLL
40 PRINT A,B
50 POKE A,B
60 LET A=A+1
70 GOTO 20
```

For this program to work, you should have a REM statement as the first line of the BASIC program with at least the same amount of characters as the length of the machine-code routine; for example, if you had a five-byte machine-code routine, you should have something like

```
1 REM 12345
```

(You could have any characters after the REM, of course—the numbers 12345 have only been included as an example.) When you come to run the loader program, enter the machine code in decimal numbers (from 0 to 255) one number at a time. The address and the value of that address are shown on screen.

Conversions of single-byte decimals to hexadecimals

	0	1	2	3	4	5	6	7	8	9	A	B	C	D	E	F
0	0	1	2	3	4	5	6	7	8	9	10	11	12	13	14	15
1	16	17	18	19	20	21	22	23	24	25	26	27	28	29	30	31
2	32	33	34	35	36	37	38	39	40	41	42	43	44	45	46	47
3	48	49	50	51	52	53	54	55	56	57	58	59	60	61	62	63
4	64	65	66	67	68	69	70	71	72	73	74	75	76	77	78	79
5	80	81	82	83	84	85	86	87	88	89	90	91	92	93	94	95
6	96	97	98	99	100	101	102	103	104	105	106	107	108	109	110	111
7	112	113	114	115	116	117	118	119	120	121	122	123	124	125	126	127
8	128	129	130	131	132	133	134	135	136	137	138	139	140	141	142	143
9	144	145	146	147	148	149	150	151	152	153	154	155	156	157	158	159
A	160	161	162	163	164	165	166	167	168	169	170	171	172	173	174	175
B	176	177	178	179	180	181	182	183	184	185	186	187	188	189	190	191
C	192	193	194	195	196	197	198	199	200	201	202	203	204	205	206	207
D	208	209	210	211	212	213	214	215	216	217	218	219	220	221	222	223
E	224	225	226	227	228	229	230	231	232	233	234	235	236	237	238	239
F	240	241	242	243	244	245	246	247	248	249	250	251	252	253	254	255

hexadecimal loader

```
    1 REM 123456789
   10 LET A=16514
   20 LET A$=""
   30 IF A$="" THEN INPUT A$
   40 IF A$(1)<"0" OR A$(1)>"F" T
HEN STOP
   50 POKE A,16*CODE A$(1)+CODE A
$(2)-476
   60 SCROLL
   70 PRINT A;TAB 10;A$( TO 2);TA
B 20;PEEK A
   80 LET A=A+1
   90 LET A$=A$(3 TO )
  100 GOTO 30
```

For this program to work, you should have a REM statement as the first line of the BASIC program with at least the same amount of characters as the length of the machine-code routine (remember that there are two digits of hex for every byte of machine code, e.g., C1 C9 occupies two bytes). When you run the loader, you can enter any amount of the machine code at a time as long as it is in complete bytes (i.e., you haven't got odd characters at the end). To stop the program, enter any character which is not a hex character, i.e., not in the range 0 to F (e.g., X or STOP). The addresses, hexadecimal values, and decimal values are displayed on the screen.

If you wish to place machine code in areas of memory other than REM statements in the first line of a BASIC program, merely replace the 16514 in line 10 of both programs with the start address of the routines.

Simulating 2K if you have more memory

If you have a RAMPACK but wish to develop a program for 2K or merely wish the display file to contract to its minimum form consisting of only ENTER characters for any reason, you can do this by altering the system variable RAMTOP to 18432 as it would be in a 2K system. Before you start this program, enter these statements as commands in the direct mode:

```
POKE 16388,0
POKE 16389,72
NEW
```

(The first statement is not usually required because 16388 normally has a value of 0.)

Postscript

WHAT DO THESE PROGRAMS DO?

```
10 FAST
20 SLOW
30 GOTO 10
```

```
10 SLOW
20 FAST
30 GOTO 10
```

Is that what's called SAVEing the best until last?

INDEX

ABOUT THE AUTHORS

TIM HARTNELL is the editor of *ZX Computing*, one of Britain's leading computer magazines. He has written a number of books on the Sinclair and other computers, and is founder/coordinator of the National ZX Users' Club, a group with over 10,000 computer-user members worldwide. He also edits the club's monthly magazine, *Interface*. Tim's background is in radio (he was a disc jockey in Australian commercial radio for five years) and television (he read news for two years). He recently edited the weekly London-based newspaper *Australasian Express* and continues to contribute a weekly column to this publication.

DILWYN JONES is a technician in the Welsh broadcasting industry. His interest in computer programming was sparked by the release of the Sinclair computer in Britain, and he has made a special study of ways of stretching this machine to its limits. He shares many of his findings in this book. Dilwyn runs a users group for T/S 1000 users in North Wales.

We Deliver!

And So Do These Bestsellers.

MONEY TALKS!
How to get it and How to keep it!